of Babaji

Maile
Hoping this little book blows your mind!
Love
Sondra!

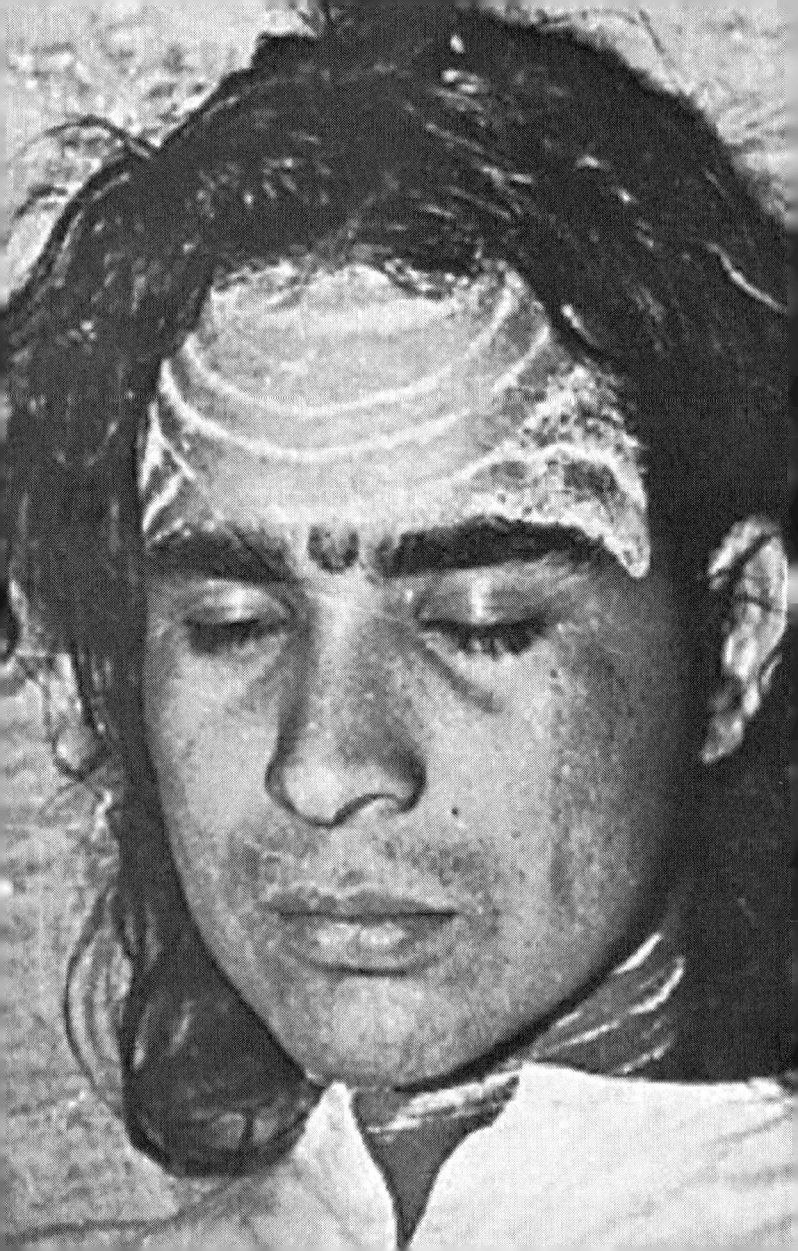

The Perfection of Babaji

Sondra Ray

with

Markus Ray

Immortal Ray Productions
Nashville   Washington D.C.

Copyright © 2020 by SONDRA RAY & MARKUS RAY

All rights reserved. No part of this publication may be reproduced, distributed or transmitted in any form or by any means, including photocopying, recording, or other electronic or mechanical methods, without the prior written permission of the publisher, except in the case of brief quotations embodied in critical reviews and certain other noncommercial uses permitted by copyright law. For permission requests, write to the publisher, addressed "Attention: Permissions Coordinator," at the address below.

Immortal Ray Productions
301 Tingey Street SE
Washington D.C. 20003
www.SondraRay.com

Immortal Ray Productions
Nashville   Washington D.C.

For bookstores, contact Immortal Ray Productions on the above website's "Contact Us" for orders of 10 or more copies.

Book and Cover Design by Markus Ray
Painting "Babaji of Denmark" on front cover.
Photo of "Babaji and Sondra Ray" on back cover.

ISBN: 978-1-950684-04-5 (paperback)
ISBN: 978-1-950684-05-2 (e-book)

Dedication

The great font of Absolute Love pours Itself across the Cosmos all pervasively forever and ever. There was no time in which this great outpouring of Creation was not. Out from the Great Void into the Great Light it poured and poured. It never stopped in extending Its Peace and Joy to every atom, every creature, every element in the great dance of all galaxies. Into this ever glorious Divine Substance is made manifest a Son from the Divine Mother and Holy Father as ONE. This Being—Greater than the Light of a thousand suns and stars—is Babaji. He is our Father, Mother and Child as One. He is our Teacher and our Friend. He is our Brother, our Sister, our Companion on this journey through the physical manifestation of Life. He is our All in the dimension beyond form, in the Infinite Spirit Realms of Divine Elation. He is higher than the High, and lower than the Low. Never absent, He is our Everything. May we bow down to touch His feet, and thus place our own Being beyond the Stars along with Him. May this surrender be a true melding of our hearts with the Universal Heartbeat of the Cosmos, the Divine Mother. May we honor all life forms that come our way, and give blessings to all. Bole Baba Ki Jai !!

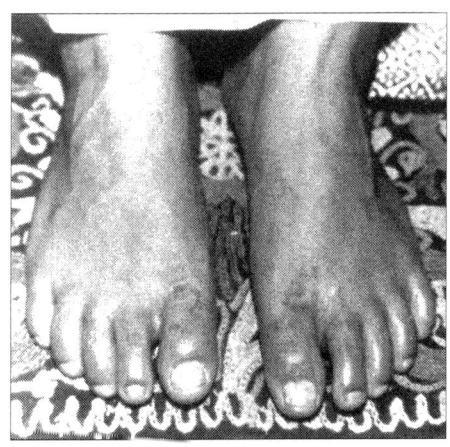

Contents

Dedication —6
Preface —10
Foreword —16

The Perfection of Babaji —28

- ◆ The thrill of having Babaji in everyday life —28
- ◆ Babaji speaks to me, "Never go back. Go to California." —28
- ◆ Shaving my head —33
- ◆ Babaji in Bali —33
- ◆ Channeling the God Training —34
- ◆ Meeting the white-haired man —36
- ◆ Babaji calls me to India —38
- ◆ Babaji in Bombay —40
- ◆ Going to Wapi —41
- ◆ Healing my "money case" —43
- ◆ Meeting Babaji as a clown —47
- ◆ What if leaving could be a joy? —53
- ◆ Miracle from Babaji in Assisi —55
- ◆ Fire purification —56
- ◆ Babaji's blessing on my world tour —58
- ◆ Gaining "Absolute Certainty" —59
- ◆ Being thrown to the lions —61

- ◆ Instructions from Babaji in Machu Picchu —63
- ◆ Babaji's samadhi and a blue cross —65
- ◆ Babaji coming to me in Toronto —66
- ◆ Resurrecting the dead —68
- ◆ Spontaneous registration —69
- ◆ Meeting an Immortalist in Canada —70
- ◆ How the Perfection of Babaji helped me find Markus, my "Twin Flame" —71
- ◆ Babaji sends healing to Markus in New Zealand —77
- ◆ Latvia miracle ! —78
- ◆ Moving to Nashville with a Babaji miracle —79
- ◆ Babaji sends us to Washington —81

You Cannot "Make Me Up" —85
The Master Is Beautiful —92

1. From Light Out of A Cave —96
2. Truth, Simplicity, Love and Service —103
3. Earth, Air, Fire, Water and Space —110

Meeting a Spiritual Master Like Babaji —115
The Perfection of the Aarti —122

Books by Sondra Ray & Markus Ray —141
Resources —205

Preface

If this book is in your hands, it means Babaji is also available to you. He always said, "My love is Available. You can take it or not." I say, why not? We need all the help we can get, no? This little book is about how Babaji worked on perfecting me and my life in my daily experience. I wrote an earlier book about Babaji which was mostly my experience at his ashram. That is truly profound and it is called *Babaji, My Miraculous Meetings with a Maha Avatar.* It also contains Markus' paintings of Babaji and poetry to Him. This little book, on the other hand, is more about how He worked with me outside the ashram in my daily life.

I had grown up in a little village in Iowa, population 300 to be exact. Markus said when I took him there, "It's in an ocean of corn," (as the cornfields go on for miles). I was raised a strict Lutheran. I knew nothing about Indian Masters in my early days, nor when I was married to my first husband. As a child I always wanted to *be perfect*, but I always felt I fell short. I remember when my Mom would say, "I don't know why you are crying when you get an 'A' minus. I am not insisting you get perfect 'As.' " Then in high school my basketball team won 34 straight games, and my number was 34. We got all the way to the state championship tournament and we lost by one point. Again, I was *not perfect* and I cried. In college I did really well except for Nutrition class. I could not get an "A" because I had so much trauma about food, having been born on the kitchen table and having had a mother who was a home economics teacher (which got me stuck on too many rules about food). After college I got married and the marriage failed after seven years, so then I really felt not perfect then. I was devastated.

When, by a miracle, I got to Rebirthing in California and became one of the first Rebirthers in the world, I learned about what we called "personal lies." This thought is your most dominant negative thought structure about yourself. Mine was for sure, "I am not perfect." I wrestled with that thought for years, and I did not understand why it kept coming up. One day I figured out that the personal lie is an actual "addiction." Perhaps I had that thought many life times. Nothing I tried seemed to help me with this addiction. It kept coming up. It took me forever to figure out why it was so hard for me to let go of it. One day I woke up and realized that in the Lutheran Church it is considered blasphemy to think you are perfect. What happens once you have committed blasphemy? Well, you die. So then, if I were to give up that thought, "I am not perfect," and chose to think I was perfect, I might actually die. This was terrifying. I think I had a harder time with "personal lies" than even my students—because of this heavy religious dogma. People who try to give up smoking know how hard that is. I felt the same with this situation. There was only one hope for me that I could see, and that was receiving the help of my Master Babaji.

For many years I had the habit of writing my woes to Babaji and putting the letters under the altar cloth under His picture. This worked for me. I knew He was getting this telepathically. Although it was very embarrassing to write out "my case" all the time, I figured one benefit of having a Master is you can bear your soul to Him. So I carried on writing Him my woes with this issue, with my affirmations to counteract my negativity, and with my prayers. Sometimes I would even write him twice a day!! I had to write, "I am perfect, alive, safe and free," over and over. I would also write, "I allow You to undo all my wrong thinking," and, "I lay my fear of perfection at Your feet." For times when I miscreated stuff and felt imperfect again I would write, "Even though I made a mistake, I still love and accept myself."

Fortunately my Guru blessed me with the ability to have a long life or else I would have been discouraged, having spent so much time stuck in imperfections. He is my example of a Perfect Master, and it is such a blessing to be connected to that—I hope you will allow yourself to also have His blessings. If you can come to India with us (bit.ly/QuestsRay) you would obviously be closer and closer to Him. But for now you can order His picture on line and set up an altar and begin your own communication to Him. Or you can just carry this little book, *The Perfection of Babaji,* around with you. It is like a small darshan, or a communion wafer that can give you His direct Presence. It's my *divine desire* you are inspired by these pictures and stories—through which I hope you get the magnificence of His perfection.

Foreword

Sondra Ray asked me to set up this book on the fly. As often happens in our household, some glint of inspiration grows brighter and brighter until it just cannot be ignored. As much as we try to "test it" and put it through the paces of a discerning eye, or a healthy dose of creative discrimination, if the skeptical "ruling out" ends and the thing is still there, it merits an action. Well, here I am, putting this "thing together"—***The Perfection Of Babaji.*** She also mentioned a "little book" would be best, one we can actually give away sometimes to inspire people to find out more about Babaji. I thought this was a good idea.

It is probably no accident either that *imperfection*, one of the perennial obsessions of the human psyche, is up to be totally dismissed and undone. Only a Master such as Babaji could do it. It's a big task. We throw Him problem after problem, glitch after glitch, and disbelief after disbelief, rejecting the Perfection in which we ourselves were created—and He dissolves all of this nonsense in just one gaze of the eye. He will knock us down silly with one look as long as we want to hang on to any remnant of reason to justify our "not being perfect." Baloney He would say to those thoughts. "Get behind me Satan," would He command the limitations of our ego beliefs to be banished forever.

Consider the thought "I am not perfect," dissolved for eternity. Is it not a "blasphemy" upon the Divinity of the human soul to insist upon our perennial imperfections? *The Perfection of Babaji* dissolves them, and proves them unworthy for even a millisecond of consideration. "Let GO and let GOD," just means claim your own *Perfection now*. Claim the immortal nature of your Real Self now. Do not delay. Do not waste time in dreams of imperfection or death. Don't allow any other thought to rule your mind but the real Thought of God, Who put Perfection at the base of your Being. What is so, just is so. What is created perfect in the beginning remains so throughout its eternal extension. Babaji is an eternal extension of Perfection, but so are you. We are no less or more Perfect than Babaji. The only difference is He is certain of his Perfection, and, well—maybe we are not so certain. We still have doubt to undo; guilt can grip us in the aftermath of mistakes; anger can take us over in the fear of the moment; frustration around an unfulfilled life issue can seem paramount in our mental world. How long are we going to insist upon holding these illusions?

The Perfection of Babaji is the subject of this book, and Sondra Ray took it on to "get it across." Well, we all grapple with what we call in Liberation Breathing our "personal lie." This is our most dominant negative thought about ourselves held in our subconscious mind, lifetime after lifetime. It ruins our flow, limits our potential, and sabotages our actions. Everyone has one to some degree. A few have naturally risen above it unaware. But for most an active look to "own the thing," and a constant vigilance to "release the thing" from our subconsciousness is needed. It can be a sobering journey. "The thing" is persistent merely from the fact we have been thinking it for so long it has become a kind of bad habit of a "personal belief." The thought "I am not perfect" is one of these "personal lies" some people have. It could go all the way back to their birth script. If a woman was not wanted as girl, and the parents intensely desired a boy, she could have this thought, "I am not perfect as a girl."

But *what is so* is so. The Perfection of what is so transcends all thoughts of the ego. God does not create "imperfect entities."

What is so is so—God created us Perfect. So the return to Love is merely a return to our own God Given Perfection. Love and Perfection go together. Love casts out the "mis-beliefs" manifesting as imperfections. Babaji helps cast out our cause and effect dynamics of attracting undesirable results in our life from maintaining the thought, "I am not perfect." He is here to totally engulf us in His Perfection, and by the principle of "right association," we then enter into the force field of our own Perfection. What could be better? Babaji has the Power to lift us out of our hell we made and place us in the Elysian Fields of Perfection just in front of Heaven's Gate. He prepares us to walk through that Gate. Will we? Well—that is yet to be decided.

This book is here to help us decide. It is here to take us to Heaven on the wings of Sri Babaji. He has soared beyond the lower levels of human suffering and its causes, and comes to fetch us out of the dangers of death and destruction. These were brought about by maintaining our self-imposed limitations, and thinking our "personal lies." *The Perfection of Babaji* is always here, but the problem is we are absent to receive it. Why? Do we think we do not deserve it? Do we think we "need to be punished" for a deep-seeded guilt we are carrying around from an ancient past of imagined separation? How long will we isolate ourselves in our own misery by insisting we are not Perfect?

In 1977 Sondra Ray met Sri Babaji in the flesh. He called her "Mrs. Sondra" for days. Then he gave her the name "Durkulai," which means, "Strong one, immortal, and everlasting." I would say She is that. And now the ante is upped. The stakes are higher now. We all must embrace our own Perfection. We all must put away the childish toys with sharp edges that would try cutting into our sacred Self that is Infallible. We all exist truly in the Infallibility of Perfection beyond our personal thoughts. We are more than our memories of conflicts, problems, and a collection of human shortcomings. Forgiveness erases them. We abide where our Divine Creator has placed us, in the life we share with the Perfection of the Universe and all living things. We have to forgive ourselves and others completely for everything, and wake up from this dream of imperfections into the Reality of the Light of Self Identity. It is one short step away in our surrender to *The Perfection of Babaji,* which is our own Perfection made manifest.

The Perfection of Babaji is the balm on the wounds of time that promises to heal our scars completely, and take us to the Diamond Body of our Spiritual counterpart. As Above so Below, and so it is that the Perfection of Divine Order can send its blessings to this earth plane and make our time and space here a much different perception. To look on a forgiven world is to look with the eyes of Babaji. He is behind our own eyes, banishing all of our mistakes, and banishing all of the mistakes we may see in others. They are just mere mirrors of our own. We are released in tandem then, with all of our brothers and sisters at once.

May this little book on *The Perfection of Babaji* be one that you carry over hill and dale, in your car or on your scooter, in your purse or backpack, on your Kindle or e-reader. Of itself it can do nothing. But melded with Babaji and your innermost workings of your own soul, it can restore your Perfection faster than, well—the swiftest thought traveling faster than the speed of Light. That would be Babaji's speed. That would be Babaji's Grace bestowed upon us. That would be *The Perfection of Babaji* awakening in our own. What Marianne Williamson once said about Sondra's book called *Pele's Wish* could be also applied to this work that "*continues the bold, wonderful saga of Sondra Ray's journey into Spirit. She makes everything we long for seem possible. We are very lucky to have her in our midst.*" —*Marianne Williamson*—

It is through *The Perfection of Babaji* that we have her in our midst. She has served Him in over seven lifetimes, we have been told. Sondra Ray and Sri Babaji go way, way back. So now it is time for this Great Sage to be recognized more widely in *our midst*—and the Perfection of His Voice in the Western World to be recognized as well, in the voice who has represented Him for over 40 years, in her life and writings—in *The Perfection of Sondra Ray.*

—Markus Ray—
Washington DC
14—January—2020

The Perfection of Babaji

The Perfection of Babaji

The thrill of having Babaji in everyday life

As I mentioned, I wrote a bigger book about Babaji with Markus called *Babaji, My Miraculous Meetings with a Maha Avatar.* It is super interesting, but most of what I wrote about in that book occurred in India at the ashram. I wanted to write a new book about what it is like to have him in one's ordinary life. It is certainly the most interesting relationship I have ever experienced, and such a Joy to have Him directing all major aspects of our life.

Babaji speaks to me, "Never go back. Go to California"

It is thrilling to recall how He turned my life around starting right in the USA. So these are stories how He has guided me outside of India for the most part. It all started just when I was ready to go back to my Ex-husband and "try again". It was two years after my divorce and when he asked me to come back, I decided I should do that. I was in Arizona and he was in Florida. I was leaving the next day. Sitting on the floor of my apartment talking to a friend on the carpet there with me, I was sharing how I felt—when suddenly we both heard a voice in the air. It was definitely NOT in my head—because he heard it also. The voice said very loudly, "NEVER GO BACK." I was immediately filled with light and could not move. Then the voice got louder and said, "NEVER GO BACK. GO TO CALIFORNIA NOW."

My friend looked at me and said, "Sondra, I think you better go to California." I replied, "If I don't follow this Voice I will regret it my whole life." I had no idea who was talking to me, but it was my first real mystical experience. I know now it was Babaji. The problem was this: I had just spent all my money on a trip to Europe. Furthermore, the California Nurses Association had written to me saying that they did not care if I had my master's degree, the waiting time for a nursing job in California was two years!

So there I was with almost no money and no hope of getting a job. But I had to go. I got in my sports car the next day and headed for California. I have no memory of crossing the desert; but when I got to the California line I started feeling really good. The sign said Los Angeles to the south and San Francisco to the north. I knew no one in California, but I decided then and there to go to San Francisco because I had read about a group doing some prenatal research I was interested in. I thought maybe they would hire me. Things started flowing miraculously. I was being guided by some force.

Driving upon the hills in San Francisco was daunting. But my car went "dead" in the Marina, right where I saw a sign that said, "furnished apartment for rent." I definitely needed that. It was on "Scott Street," which was my married name at the time. I banged on the manager's door and told him I needed to live there. He gave me the price of rent and deposit and I was shocked at the amount, and definitely did not have that. I told him I didn't have that much money, but insisted I needed to live there. We kept going back and forth with the same debate. He finally said, "I don't know what is about you lady, but I will let you move in. I have not done that for 25 years." Then I shocked even myself by saying, "I will get a job tomorrow."

I went to the place where they were doing research and they told me they did not have the funds to hire me—but maybe they could help me get a job. They made one phone call, and right then I got the job at Kaiser Hospital in the prenatal clinic! (That turned out to be the right place for my future life as a Rebirther.) After a few weeks I was led to meeting Leonard Orr who was doing a new experiment he called Rebirthing. I was one of the first people he tried it on and all my problems cleared up! I became one of the first Rebirthers in the world and am still doing that all over the globe. Who else but Babaji could have arranged such a miracle?

And yet it was a long time before I knew who was talking to me. When we went to India and found our guru Babaji in 1977, I knew it was Him who had been guiding me. My life unfolded so beautifully. I could not have imagined it myself.

Shaving my head for the first time.

The first time I shaved my head to surrender to Babaji, I came home and landed in Los Angeles. The friends who met me at the airport said they wanted to take me to this movie called "Altered States." I told them I was already in an altered state—but anyway, "Let's go!" In the middle of the movie I left my body and heard Babaji say to me : "You must do *The God Training*. It is not a question of can you do it or will you do it, this must be done." I said, "Okay," and came crashing back into my body wondering what on earth I had agreed to. I just could not seem to get it for a whole year—so I finally told my staff I was going to Bali, the Island of the Gods, and I was not coming back until I got *The God Training*.

Babaji in Bali

Babaji guided me the whole time in Bali. The first night I stayed at the lovely Oberoi

Hotel. But I could only afford that for one night at that time. The second morning I was walking down a path with my suitcase wondering where I would go to spend the weeks ahead. A kind Balinese man stopped me and asked if I wanted a guide. I certainly did! He took me to Poppie's Cottages near Kuta Beach which were very affordable and near the beach. Every single day after that, the man would cross town on his motorbike and bring me offerings his family made for my altar. This went on for 6 weeks when I was there. I could not have arranged that by myself. I was so grateful for this time of total Divine Care. I fell in love with Bali and have been going back every year with Markus since 2010 to take people on the Bali Quest (bit.ly/BQRay).

Channeling the God Training

While I was at Poppie's Cottages for the first time, I channeled *The God Training* in just 15 minutes. Right then, I looked out my window—and parading by were one hundred women in gorgeous batiks, carrying headdresses of holy offerings of all kinds—of fruits that were piled in such a way that I couldn't believe they were not falling off. I had never dreamed I would see such a beautiful sight. So, feeling really proud of myself for getting how to do *The God Training*, I followed them. They walked down to the beach and kneeled down and put batik cloths on the beach for an altar. Then they kneeled down and carefully placed the baskets of fruits on this altar. I finally found someone to explain this to me. She said, "You are so lucky to see this. Today is the day they all pray for families on the island." Imagine that. I will never forget this day.

Every day I would read *A Course in Miracles*. I outlined the Text of *ACIM* to be used as a study guide called, *Drinking the Divine* (bit.ly/DrinkingRay). That got me pretty high. Sometimes I would sit at the restaurant of my villa and order black rice pudding, which I really liked.

Meeting the white haired man

One day something amazing happened. It could only have been Babaji, although I did not get that at the time. A very unusual man was suddenly at the restaurant. He had pure white hair, which later I found very unusual as he was young. He said the following to me:

A clairvoyant told me I was going to meet you here.

I was too surprised to ask him how he knew my name, etc. He said he was an actor, and he wanted me to come to Perth, Australia, and Rebirth all his friends. (And how did he know I was a Rebirther?) Again, I was too surprised to ask that. I told him I could not do that as I would be in Bali for a few more weeks. He then told me to do two things:

1) Go to Monkey Forest Road in Ubud and find such and such a high priest and have his body work.
2) Go to such and such a restaurant and order #14 on the menu.

I found the priest the next day and he did every type of body work on me, which was extraordinary. After I got up I felt so amazing that I had to sit on the ground. I said to myself, "I never knew I could feel this good."

When I found the restaurant, I was shocked that it was a tiny little place and no one was in there. So I ordered #14 on the menu, like the white haired man said to do. They then served me this soup with little dark mushrooms floating on top. I said to myself, "What if these were magic mushrooms?" Then I decided that that was ridiculous because how would they ever have that in a restaurant on the menu? So I ate it all.

Boy, was I in for a surprise. My intuition was right. I was flying and seeing Jesus. That week I was staying with a Balinese family because Poppie's Cottages were fully booked. I must have made a noise, because all of a sudden a dashing young Balinese man was sitting on my bed asking me if I was okay. I remember his teeth were filed straight and he was stunning. He said, "I want to make sure you are all right. Do you want me to stay and make love to you?" Now I could not believe that. I turned him down but who was he? I had never seen him in that family before. After this experience I totally surrendered to Bali and I was more or less in bliss the whole time.

Babaji calls me to India

When I was nearing the end of my stay, Babaji appeared to me in a dream wearing all red and motioning for me to come toward Him. When I got up that morning, there was an actual telegram in my door and it was from Babaji. It said, "Come to India. Don't come to Haidakhan (His ashram) but meet me in Bombay."

How could it be that the telegram was there, signed "Babaj?" No one knew where I was! Now, I had no plans to go to India and I certainly did not have a visa. So I found out I had to go to Singapore to get that. In order to do that I had to get a cholera shot in Bali. That night I got the shot, but I also contracted a dose of cholera. I was so sick I could not move and the lights went out, due to a rain storm. Then flies were landing all over my body. They had not been out so profusely before. I remember saying, "I have become a carcass." Miraculously, I was healed by 7AM the next morning, and someone came and took me to the airport.

In Bombay the movie *Ghandi* had just come out, so I met Leonard Orr (the founder of Rebirthing) and dragged him to the movie. That film is amazing! (I have now seen it four times.) That night I could not sleep. I could feel Babaji coming down from the mountains and He was pushing my death urge up and out. I was terrified I was going to die before He got there!

Babaji in Bombay

Babaji was touring Bombay visiting His rich devotees there. I was invited by Him on this tour, much to my amazement. I was staying with a wealthy couple who had seven servants. Every day we would get up at 3AM and drive across the city to be with Babaji where He was giving darshan. There was a huge tent filled mostly with hundreds of Indian devotees. There were few westerners.

I was sitting in the back. One day Babaji came out wearing a white silk garment with a fuchsia velvet sash. I was swooning. I loved His fashion. Suddenly He took the sash off and threw it to me. Now mind you, it went over rows and rows of people, by the hundreds, without falling down—and landed in my lap!

Another day He called me up front of everyone and said my name out loud like a mantra, over and over, and then He put all kinds of energy around me. He began to dance around me singing, "Sondra Ray! Sondra Ray! Sondra Ray!" It was exhilarating, but I kind of knew the "shit was going to hit the fan," and I was in for a huge process. I knew something was going to happen and He was preparing me for it.

Going to Wapi

We used to be afraid of Him, and what He might order us to do. Like, I used to think, "Wow, what if He tells me to move to China or something?" On this particular day He said to me, "You go to Wapi." I had no idea where that was or how to get there. So I asked around, and I found out that it was a farm in a town not too far away called Wapi. This farm was kind of an *ashram,* and Babaji had more or less adopted the whole town of Wapi, as it was very poor.

I managed to get a ride. When we got there I was thrilled because I was going to be living in the same house as Babaji. But then I could hardly handle that. Babaji told me, "You sleep on the kitchen floor." I could not believe it, as the floor was packed mud and had little hamsters running around eating up the potato peelings, etc. Then it dawned on me that Babaji was once again processing me on my birth trauma as I was born in the kitchen. Needless to say I did not sleep well at all, and I got a severe headache which is the only time I came close to experiencing what a migraine must be like. It was brutal.

In the morning Babaji was in the living room swinging in a swing (He loved swings). He was laughing and throwing water on everyone. I was miserable. I wanted to leave—to escape. I said to Him in my mind,

"Babaji, I cannot stand this pain. You have to help me or I have to leave India now." Suddenly, someone gave Him a silver tray with silver glasses on it. He said, "Some of you need this," looking straight at me. I figured it was some herbal tea. It tasted very bitter, and so I did not drink much at all.

Healing my "money case"

After that, I realized I had forgotten to cash in my traveler's checks and I had no money. I went to find my shoes but they were stolen. I didn't have another pair either, as we were only there for two nights. So there I was walking down to the town bare footed, looking for a bank. I suddenly started feeling really poor like a poor Indian. Then it would switch, and I would feel like a very rich American. Back and forth this went.

I was getting woozy, but not yet realizing there was something in that drink. (I think it was datura plant or something.)

The banks kept telling me, "This is not Bombay—we don't cash travelers checks here." I went outside, after a few banks, and grabbed a rickshaw. I asked the driver to take me to a bank where they would cash them. He started driving me out in the country. I was getting more woozy now, and my headache was starting to lift. Sure enough, there was a bank out there in the country, but it was not open. I could not figure out why this bank was not open, and the ones in town were open. So I sat on the grass waiting. I was now facing the fact that I was on some kind of psychedelic plant. I started breathing heavily, kind of rebirthing myself.

An old man came and told me I could go in the bank. There were no tellers or cleaners in there, and no lights were turned on. Just me. That was odd. Suddenly I felt myself in a full on Rebirthing session, hyperventilating. I could feel Babaji entering my body and pushing me. I would alternate saying, "Take it easy on me and back off," and then I would say, "No, just sock it to me!"

Finally it happened. I remembered a past life where I was killed in a bank. My mother used to say I never had any fear except in banks, and she could never understand that. Babaji took me through the whole memory and then when it was over. The lights came on and the tellers came in, and the really amazing thing was two Babaji devotees from the farm where there to fetch me. They said, "Oh Sondra, do you need any help?" I said, "You might say so—I am trying to cash these travelers checks." They assisted me in doing that. I was relieved !

Then, these two German devotees took me back to the farm, which was great, because I had no idea where I was, or where the farm was. I felt like I was inside out. Babaji called us to come with Him to the center of the village where he was feeding everyone. There were thousands. I just laid back in the truck. I still could not move. Later the man in charge told me there was only food for one thousand people available, but somehow over two thousand people were fed! Go figure.

Later, a messenger came to my room that evening saying Babaji wanted me to attend his private fire ceremony at 3AM. Now, "This is a real honor to be invited to that," I thought. It is done in total silence. I got up early to prepare myself to meet Him. It was just Babaji and me in His room. At one point He looked right at me across from the fire, and I heard Him say to me telepathically, "You finally got through it," meaning my *money case.* I knew in that instant that He had saved me decades of clearing on my money karma. My process in the bank was orchestrated entirely by Him! What perfection! Big tears flew out of my eyes horizontally toward Him. That was the last time I saw Him in person.

Meeting Babaji as a clown

I decided to do the first *God Training* at Mt. Shasta, California, as I knew it was the "home" of St. Germain, the immortal master of the United States. The night before I left to go there a woman from Alaska, who was coming, called me to say that she had a dream Babaji would show up there. I said, "Oh great," thinking that He would appear in a vision to someone while they were having a Rebirthing session. (This often happens.)

At the end of the training I was approached by a student who told me he was going to the post office to get his magic mushrooms. I said, "You are getting that in the mail? I want to go with you and see this." I was in for some fun. But I told him it was Saturday, and the post-office would be closed. He said, "No, the package department will be open." I went along and sure enough it was. We got in line.

Standing in front of me was this crazy looking clown who reminded me of the Simpsons. He had orange hair and was wearing a plaid shirt and striped pants with suspenders. The weird thing was that the stripes did not line up. In other words, the bottom part of the stripes did not line up with the top part of the stripes going down. I was thinking, "What fabric maker would make such a fabric?" I was freaking out! Then the clerk was handing him back a package and said to him, "This is not readable."

I peered over his shoulder and saw the letters shaking on the package. It was then I started confronting this clown. I said, "Who do you think could read this?" He nudged me with his elbow saying, "Don't worry, it's Egyptian." What an off the wall statement. Then he turned around and faced me, and showed me his palm. There were absolutely no lines on his palm. I was astounded.

He said to me, "I know Dennis A. you know." I said startled, "YOU know Dennis?" (That was my boyfriend at the time.) He then said, "Yes, and I know Yogananda too." That should have been a clue to me that this was Babaji appearing to me in disguise. Because Yogananda wrote the book *Autobiography of a Yogi*, and Chapters 33& 34 are about Babaji. However, I could not think straight.

Suddenly He had me in the corner and He was putting His face up to mine saying, "Gaines!" four times. I said, "What is this, the thought of the day?" "No," he said. "It is my name." Now, that should have been another clue because Babaji used to say things to me in India four times if he really wanted me to get it. I could feel myself going out of my body.

Then he said, "I am making a movie you know." I said, "YOU? You are making a movie? What is it about?" He replied, "I can't tell you yet."

All of a sudden I was in the car and did not remember getting in. As we drove off I yelled, "Stop the car! That was Babaji appearing to me in disguise!" I ran back in to find Him, but He was gone. Then I started laughing and laughing all the way back to the resort.

When we got there Gaines was already there, and He was on the swinging bridge having a debate about UFOs with Dennis. As I approached, He yelled, "Here comes the Virgo," (meaning me). How did He know that? I had not told him. Then I would lose my mind again and forget everything.

Suddenly He had a whole family—a wife and two kids, and they all looked kind of like the Simpsons. I could not believe my eyes. Only a very few people saw this, and we all were Babaji devotees. In a flash the "family" was all up on the terrace having breakfast. Dennis and I were getting ready to go to Eugene, Oregon, to teach a healing seminar.

I felt so exposed and wanted to run out of there as fast as I could. It was nearly too much for me. Then Gaines yelled toward us, "I'll see you guys in Eugene." How did He know that was where we were going next? Again, He seemed to be able *to see right into me.*

For a couple of years I told no one about this because I was sure they would not believe it. If Babaji had appeared to me looking the same as He did in India, I would have fainted, because I would have known I was experiencing bi-location. He *was* in India at the time. I *was* experiencing bi-location. But because He was in disguise I did not get it full on, otherwise I would have really freaked out. He knew how much I could handle, so His "clown disguise" was part of His Perfection.

A few years later I was in Melbourne, Australia, leading a chanting evening. There were about 80 people in the room and I was teaching them Om Namaha Shivay. Right before I started, a "bag lady" came through the meeting room, headed straight for me. She looked like she had been going through the garbage. Nobody saw her but me, even though she was carrying balloons. She put a doll in my lap. My thought was that maybe I needed to lighten up. Then I realized that the doll was the exact replica of Gaines, but the stripes on the pants were lined up!

After that I started sharing this story in the trainings and would show the doll. But then in Rome I had left the doll on the bed and the maid had thrown it away with the sheets. I was really upset to lose it. I couldn't seem to get off my upset even after we landed in Valencia, Spain. We went out for dinner with our organizers to a restaurant. A crazy guy came into the restaurant with stuffed animals hanging all over him. He placed a pink rabbit in front of me on our table and pushed a button. It started dancing and singing, while the ears went back and forth. Clearly the rabbit was singing, "Bring peace and joy to every girl and boy!" Was that Babaji also????   Most likely. He was showing us the real purpose of our mission together—bring Joy to the world. I have this rabbit and we let is sing occasionally, but it is too big to travel with on the road.

What if leaving could be a joy?

Once I was living with a great guy for two years and I thought we were having a great relationship. But he came home one day and shocked me by saying, "I have to leave." I asked, "Are you upset with me?" He said no. "Are you upset with our relationship?" He said no, again. He just said he had to leave and he gave no explanation. And then he left.

I was really distraught; but then I pulled it together and jumped on the plane to my next destination. I was proud of myself for letting go. But when I got there I was walking in the park bemoaning the fact that he was not with me. I could not seem to drop it. I was miserable without him. But then it happened again: I heard that Voice outside of my head. It said, "What if leaving could be a joy?" I spoke back to the Voice protesting. "That is ridiculous!" I said. The Voice once again came and said, "Just wait until you see what I have for you next!!" Ashamed of my lack of faith, I threw myself on the grass apologizing to God and Babaji.

And lo and behold that year ahead was so much better than the last, and the little life that I thought was IT. Babaji gave me everything so grand and so beautiful that I became totally aware that if I had married that man it would have been a total mistake. Once again, *The Perfection of Babaji* saved me from a bad situation, in this case being with the wrong man.

Miracle from Babaji in Assisi

The third time I heard the Voice of Babaji speaking to me was right after my mother died. I was working in Sweden at the time. The Swedes really took care of me after I found out this news. (I am half Swedish, you know.) That night they took me to a cottage on a lake where Ammachi (my female guru) spends one day a year resting. They let me sleep in Her bed, and that really, really helped me deal with my grief. I was on my way to Italy and I was developing a severe ear ache the next morning. I did NOT want to hear that bad news about my mother's death, obviously.

I went to a doctor who told me it was too inflamed to clean out. So I said, "Never mind, I will shave my head." Then I was flying off again. I went to the ashram in Italy and got a yogi to do my mundan (head shave), which is often done in India after a parent dies. Right after that, I went to the little chapel of St.

Francis near Assisi to pray. (It is in the bigger church, and is called the Portiuncula.) Sitting in the chapel I heard the words, "I AM," out loud in the air, four times. Not in my head, but outside of it. Babaji, again. My ear was healed instantly, on the spot at that moment! (As I said, Babaji often used to say some things to me four times in a row when He really wanted me to get it.)

Fire purification

Sometimes when I was way OFF and making a huge mistake, Babaji would literally start fires in my room. Once I was staying at the home of some other Rebirthers in NYC. I had my altar very far from the bed. I woke up and my bed covers were on fire! My mind cleared and I knew immediately where I was off. I had given my power away to another teacher who impressed me (because she told me she was a "walk in", and I had never met one before). Somehow I had her up on a pedestal because of that. While I was putting out the fire, I was clear that I had to take my power back, and I knew exactly how to do it.

In another *fire incident*, once I was speaking on the phone to a lover I had in Canada. The only thing I had burning was a stick of incense in a holder on the television set. Suddenly when on the call, the heavy weight curtain started burning. I knew instantly I was not to have anything more to do with that man, so I hung up abruptly and put out the fire. (Later I found out he was a "womanizer" and was very disloyal.) I was so afraid to tell the manager of the hotel about this curtain. So I went down to the office with a picture of Babaji in my hand and tried to explain the unexplainable. She was very kind and told me not to worry about it. Now there was no way that incense could have gotten over to the curtain by itself. Furthermore, the curtain was very strong thick material. It would never have caught fire by itself, even if the incense could have hit it.

Babaji's blessing on my world tour

Once I was starting my first world tour alone. I did not have any fear that I knew of. I had said to Babaji that I was willing to be totally aligned with Him. I was sitting in meditation in my hotel room in Alaska. Suddenly He appeared in an empty room, and told me to walk with Him. This was not a dream! Every step He took I took with Him, in total alignment. After that, He picked me up and hugged me. It felt like He was really there. My organizer came in the room and was stunned. "Your hair has grown suddenly!" she shouted. I told her I did not have time to explain that, as we had to get to the TV station to do an interview. My world tour was perfect. No mistakes. At the end of it, I was in Melbourne Australia. I was sitting on the floor sharing with a guy about the trip and he suddenly started bowing to me profusely. "What are you doing?" I inquired. He reported that Babaji had taken over his body to acknowledge me~!

Gaining "Absolute Certainty"

It was Christmas Eve in New York City and the city was buzzing like a continual shot of adrenaline. I was staying at a Rebirther's apartment and everyone was out and about. I was Rebirthing myself and suddenly the phone rang, and I knew it was for me. A man's voice was on the other end saying, "I know all about you. I teach *A Course in Miracles,* and I want you to come over." Ordinarily I would NEVER go to a stranger's home in New York.

I remember getting in the cab and I remember going to a brownstone and ringing the bell. A man with white hair (like the one in Bali) who looked like an angel let me in. He had the fire going in the fireplace with a mat beside it. He asked me if I minded if he called in my guides. I said, " Please do."

Then he began hypnotizing me and taking me down steps in my mind. He said, "Who is at the bottom of the steps?" I said, "Oh, it is Babaji." There He was sitting, waiting for me. "He wants me to review two past lives," I said.

In the first one I was teaching and there were a lot of men in the audience. So this guide said, "What does Babaji want you to get from that life?" "ABSOLUTE CERTAINTY," I said.

The next life I was teaching and doing a really good job, and a child was with me on the stage sitting quietly sending light. It was my child. He was very young and I was amazed he could be so still. Again, the guide asked me, "What does Babaji want you to get from reviewing that life?" I said again, "ABSOLUTE CERTAINTY." Then we were finished. I don't remember anything else. Did I really go somewhere, out into New York that night? Or was it all on another dimension? Anyway, ever since that experience I have had *absolute certainty* about my work.

Being thrown to the lions

I was working in Germany and my organizer called me and told me he was in a spontaneous Rebirthing around past lives. I told him to come over so I could give him a session. He then remembered being thrown to the lions. I told him that we must go to the zoo the next day right when it is opening before the crowds and go see the lions, and then we would go to the stadium. I was sure this would help him clear. We were the very first people going into the zoo.

A funny man came up to us and he had the largest mug of beer that I had ever seen—definitely not one you could find in a bar. (Definitely this was not normal!) And why was he drinking beer at 9AM? Furthermore, he started making sounds like all the animals, and these sounds came out perfectly—they sounded so real—too uncanny, really. Then he said, "You see that peacock up in that tree? Peacocks cannot go that high."

(Peacocks are often around Babaji because they are immune to poison, like Lord Shiva.) I said, "What are you doing here?" He said this, "I am always here." I rushed to the lions because that guy made me nervous. But then I told my organizer I thought it was Babaji. His nose started bleeding when I said that, and he had a total purification.

Afterwards we went to the stadium and went high up in the bleachers. There was nobody there. We sat down and all of a sudden a man appeared in front of us and took our picture. It seemed so strange that we did not see him before climbing up the bleachers. Where did he come from?

Instructions in Machu Picchu from Babaji

I was taking a group to Machu Picchu, Peru. I was excited as I always had wanted to go there. The first night we stopped near Cuzco to get acclimated to the altitude. We all were going to go into the hot springs, and I was preparing them. A minister who was attending the retreat said to me that she had a severe headache, and she was seeing an amethyst in her third eye. I told her to lie down in the back and do nasal breathing. Right after that, I felt a huge block of energy moving toward me. It was so strong that I told the group that I had to lie down and start Rebirthing myself with her. The other trainer carried on talking. When we were both lying there she said, "Your guru is here." She was seeing Babaji. I asked, "What is He wearing," for some reason. She said, "A poncho." Well I thought, that is perfect for Peru. Then she told me He wanted her to take me to this cave when we got to Machu Picchu. I said, "Okay," that I would follow her.

We decided to go into Machu Picchu *after* the tourists left, and remain in silence. I don't remember how I got permission for my group to do this; but it turned out to be a very good idea. Babaji led her to the cave which was called the Cave of Auras. I was told to spend the next day in there the whole day.

I requested that my body worker come in with me in case I went through a lot. Permission granted. The rest of the group hiked up a steep mountain that day. They later reported that they saw a huge form of Babaji sitting on top of the cave. In there I got certain "instructions." One was that I was to go to Medjugorje, Croatia, and I was to go alone. This is the place where the children were seeing the visions of the Virgin Mary. I said, "Okay," but I did not really even know at the time where that was, or why I was supposed to go there. My body worker kept rocking back and forth and he seemed to be going through more than I was.

I was also given the vision of a healing center with glass steps going down, and they were very wide with different colors under each one. People were to stand on each step and get color therapy. So far I am not even close to creating that. But it was very exciting to be there in Machu Picchu, receiving these instructions from Babaji, to say the least.

I did go to Medjugorje and saw the children who were seeing the Virgin Mary. I wrote about this experience in my Book, *Inner Communion.* You can get it here: bit.ly/CommunionRay.

Babaji's Samadhi and the Blue Cross

I was holding a chanting evening at a mansion in Beverly Hills. After about an hour and a half when people were leaving to go outside. I heard them yelling for me to come out quickly. They were all looking up at the sky, and pointing to a very, very large blue cross that was right over the house. There was absolutely no explanation. But the next day I received word that Babaji had left his body at that exact time. He was obviously merging His electrons with the universe. Devotees from all over started calling me and I tried to calm them down. I was not sad at all because I knew Babaji was not really dead. He could make a new body anytime He wanted to. Babaji is omnipresent and all-knowing. I knew He knew exactly what He was doing. I told everyone, "It's time we grow up and get to work!" Any spiritual Master will want you to have your own freedom of Truth, Simplicity, Love and Service! We trust Babaji to lead us to this within our own destiny.

Babaji coming to me in Toronto

I went to Toronto to work and I was staying in the home of a Rolfer. She and her son were sleeping downstairs and I was upstairs. The first night I felt Babaji enter my body and very loud sounds came out of me. I was breathing like mad—nearly hyperventilating. The mother and son told me they heard me and wanted to come and help me; but they literally could not move. I was fine, I told them, and I said, "I was just having an exorcism." At least it felt like Babaji was pulling out of me deeper levels of my subconscious blocks. This went on for two more nights.

The next night I had a vision in which I was going to a dignitary's funeral and I had to stand in line for ages to get to the casket. When I got there it was Babaji in the casket ! He gave me the most amazing darshan with the most love I have ever felt. Then He opened His eyes and raised his hand to bless me. The amazing thing about that is He did it exactly the way my father did from his death bed, the last time I saw him alive in the hospital. (Even then, *The Perfection of Babaji* was still processing me on my past !)

The next night I had a vision that I was walking in India. The sights and smells were exactly like everything there ! It seemed I was not dreaming, but really present in India. Then Babaji came into my body so strong I told Him I had to go to my hotel room and lie down. I was up on the 11th floor it seemed. All of a sudden I saw a ravishingly beautiful woman going by my window. "Wait a minute," I said out loud, "There aren't any sidewalks up here!" Never in this life had I seen such beauty. I guess it was the Divine Mother Herself, or should I say Babaji in the form of the Divine Mother appearing to me that night, walking in the clear space of my being, outside my window.

Resurrecting the dead

The following night I had a vision where there was a very old casket in my room. (I am not even a visual person. I am more auditory.) It was all covered with cobwebs and there was a skeleton in there. Suddenly the skeleton started growing muscles and skin and became alive! It even started crawling out of the casket and walking toward me. It was Babaji ! A woman next to me said, "Sondra Ray, you are really into some heavy shit resurrecting the dead," and then she fainted. End of vision. It took me years to understand that one. Years later when I asked Shastriji about this incident, Babaji's High Priest told me, "Because of your great past lives, Babaji allowed you to see His resurrected body." What a blessing that was. And I am still integrating this in light of our teachings on Physical Immortality. It's like Babaji was showing me the real truth, that "There is no death !"

Spontaneous registrations

My next stop was Florida. I was "fried," and had to have a chiropractor work on me for over an hour. I was doing a preview for the LRT. What happened there never happened before or after. People just got up while I was talking and signed up at the registration table for the LRT. They did not even wait until I was done. Such was my energy that day.

Meeting an Immortalist in Canada

I was in working in Montreal and happened to see a newspaper that said this on the front page: "Do you want to live to be 600? The first 106 years are a snap." And there was a man there who looked about 60 claiming to be 106. Now, I knew about the immortals in the Bible, so I wanted to meet him. Monday, after the training, I found him and sat at his feet—pretending I did not know anything about Physical Immortality. So I asked him, "What is the secret?" He said, "You have to love God, love yourself, and serve humanity." Then he jumped up and down yelling, "VIVA CANADA !!!!"

His daughter was sitting nearby and she actually looked older than he did. So I interviewed her, asking her what she thought of her father. "Oh, he has so much energy he makes me feel old." She was *aging* with that thought! Then her father said he was taking a peace walk across the country, starting the next day. Now, was that Babaji appearing to me? Probably. He would definitely tell me to serve humanity.

How The Perfection of Babaji helped me find Markus, my Twin Flame !

One day I decided I wanted to experience a holy relationship in this incarnation. I told Babaji I wanted someone who would fit the mission. I could not make a mistake, would He please choose my mate? After all, He knows everyone's past, present and future. Well, I more or less asked for an *arranged marriage.* However I was so used to being independent that it did not happen immediately. I had to prepare myself.

I was teaching a money seminar in Philadelphia when it happened. Taking that training was a man I had known some twenty years back. At the end of the training I said, "Are you still an artist?" The answer was yes. "Are you still married?" The answer was no. The next day he came to me for a private session and acknowledged me for introducing him years ago to *A Course In Miracles*, to Babaji, India, Rebirthing, and to the Hawaiian *Ho'Oponopono* process. He gave me a very large tithe.

I told him I needed a new *Ho'Oponopono* book, and did he know how I could get one? He said yes, so I asked him to drive me to that place. When I got in the car, I was shocked to see he had a large photo of my kahuna teacher, Morrnah Simeona, on the dashboard. This really struck me, as in India the taxi drivers all have their guru on their dashboard like that. So he really got my attention.

After we got the book at Connie W.'s place, we walked across Rittenhouse Square to a high end fish restaurant named Devon's. My assistant, Shanti, from France was with us. At the meal I noticed that this man was very, very deep. I had not seen him for twenty years. Well, I was impressed and I put my arm interlocked with his when we were walking back across the square to his car. Later, when he dropped Shanti and me off, he gave me a book of his writings. His writing was incredibly spiritual and wonderful. In this book there were also small and intensely colorful watercolor paintings. I was stunned by their clarity and beauty.

My two girlfriends from Europe, Shanti from Paris and Diana from London, were there with me—who were also Babaji devotees. Both had come to the Philadelphia Rebirthing Center by a fluke. Their flights got rerouted etc. They both came in my room and said, "Sondra, don't you get it? He is the ONE!" It was like Babaji speaking to me saying through them, "Don't miss this window of opportunity." They really got my attention.

Well, afterwards I was headed for Ashville, N.C. to work. So on Valentine's day (Babaji's Samadhi day) I asked Markus if he wanted to come down and join me, and he said yes. He drove through a snow storm, and when he arrived at the home where I was staying the hostess said, "You will be staying in the back room with Sondra." I did not even know she said that. Both of us felt a little shy, and that things were moving quite fast.

That night we had a group Rebirthing at a center where I had given a book signing the night before. I went over to him during the breathe and said, "Well why don't you come to Nashville with me tomorrow?" He said, " I am 99% sure I can't." I said, "Well, Okay." But ½ hr. later I went back to check on his session. He said, "You know that 1%? Babaji said I would be crazy not to go for it." So Markus drove my friend and I to Nashville where I was presenting an LRT in a Unity Church! We fell in love in Nashville at the

Bluebird Café, listening to Mike Henderson playing bottleneck blues guitar!

While I was doing the group Rebirthing in the Unity Church, people were lying in the pews breathing with their heads toward the aisles. I asked my girlfriend to get up and read some of her sensual Love poetry for the closing. After listening to this, Markus got up from his Rebirth and asked me to marry him in Haidakhan (Babaji's ashram) that Spring. He had already decided to come back with me on the India Quest that year. I immediately said, "Yes, but I want to wait a year so all my girlfriends can come!" It turned out the ones I thought would come didn't, but other remarkable friends came.

So we lived and worked for a year, together in Marina Del Ray in Los Angeles. Just before coming out in March for us to go in the India Quest 2008, he called me before he arrived and said, "How would you feel if I arrived naked?" (Like, without any attachment to any of the property or financial entitlements from his "old life.") I said, "I think that would be great! I would not want any of that old energy anyway." So, Markus left everything behind and showed up with two suitcases, and nothing else. He had a couple really nice leather jackets, a set of Henkel Kitchen Knives and his most prized possessions—a few choice books and journals. That began our real life and mission together in March of 2008. We have been together 24/7/365 ever since.

We got married around the Havan (fire ceremony) on April 4, 2009, the last day of Navaratri, the nine day festival to the Divine Mother in Haidakhan. We were told Babaji would "show up," and he did in the form of Sri Muniraj. He came down from his private quarters to give us a blessing, which he never did before for others getting married. Our marriage has been one big miracle all the time, ever since then. Now my husband is my miracle and Babaji guides us together. *The Perfection of Babaji* flows through us and inspires us on a daily basis, and we work hard in that Pure Joy.

Babaji sends healing to Markus in New Zealand

It was Markus' birthday and we were walking on the beach in New Zealand with our organizer, Patricia. Markus has always been a bit self-conscious of his skin condition, as he has a mild form of vitiligo. On this day, a lady came up to us who had this condition severely all over her body. She was very, very happy. She also had a crazy dog with her named George. Later we were out in a random café restaurant a few miles from the beach, and the same lady showed up there too. It seemed surreal. After we waited in line to order our coffee, then sat down to be served, she came and served us—not the waitress! She and George brought our coffee over and thanked us for being there. There was in a state of Pure Joy, and her joy was contagious. We all felt blessed and delighted in her presence. And then almost instantly, she and George disappeared. I really felt it was Babaji, because of the energy, and she seemed to want to heal Markus from his last bits of self-consciousness around his skin condition.

Latvia miracle !

Some of the ways Babaji works in our lives don't seem like such big miracles compared to what I have written so far. However, I credit Him for the smaller miracles. Such as, we were in Latvia and I was disappointed that our organizer was not going to work out. He did not want to do it again. But there was a tall entrepreneur in the training who bought the painting of Babaji that Markus painted during the seminar. After he went home, he sent us a text to invite us to dinner. We got together with him and his wife, who is a wonderful clairvoyant and Breathworker. They are very spiritual, and extremely tapped into Babaji's

Energy, even though they have not been to Haidakhan. They have a number of children and she is a writer as well. He, like Markus had done years ago, works as a builder.

Half way through the dinner they offered to organize for us in the summer of 2020. We were delighted to still be able to work in Latvia. Babaji took one person out, not aligned with His Energy, and immediately put two people in his place—people totally in His Vibe! Markus was marveling at *The Perfection of Babaji* in this reboot of our work in Latvia! I thought that sounded like a great book title. So here it is now. THANK YOU, Janis and Evita, for flowing with this perfection in all your glory! We can't wait to work with you and be with you for a long period, over time, with a deep Holy Relationship!

Moving to Nashville with a Babaji miracle

We were living in Marina Del Rey, California, as I said, for the first year of being together.

When we got married in India, we went to Thailand for our honeymoon where a very powerful Babaji devotee has built a wellness spa, Kamalaya, that always gets the "Best Wellness Spa" awards for Asia. Before our wedding, we had got the guidance to move to Nashville, the city where we fell in love. Our Breathwork community there supported us in this move. It was at the time a lovely city with low costs. A real simple place to be, compared to Los Angeles. The amazing thing that happened was that some of our students picked out an apartment for us, sight unseen by us. We trusted them, and it turned out to the perfect place for our new home! And not only that, they met the moving truck with all our furniture on it—they unpacked all the boxes and everything, and decorated our place better than we could have—while we were on our honeymoon! We did not have to lift a finger. One gal was an artist, so they even hung our art. When we came home from Thailand everything was in place, perfectly unpacked and arranged. We did not have to redo anything. A real Babaji miracle!

Babaji sends us to Washington

We were living the quiet life in Nashville, still travelling a lot, however. We lived there for eight years and loved every minute of it. When we came home, life was easy. At the end of 2016, right after Trump was elected President, we were leading the Bali Quest and at the end, after it was over, we were lying down relaxing—listening to *Buddha Bar* music (our favorite). Suddenly I heard in my head, "MOVE TO WASHINGTON D.C." This would have never ever occurred to me, so I was stunned. I turned to Markus and told him what I had heard and he remarked, "I just heard that too." So in that moment we realized it was our new assignment and Babaji was giving it to us. We surrendered immediately, even though we were both surprised. So, I told Markus that we better shave our heads and maybe we should do it at the temple of death, Gunung Kawi, which is in the "bowels" of Bali. After all, we were working on our book at the time, *Physical Immortality*, and we wanted to remove any of our *unconscious death urge* that still may have been in us (bit.ly/ImmortalRay). I thought we better process more death programming so we went there. You have to walk down 400 steps, down into the lower levels of the Temple. Markus had never been there, but he wanted to see it. So we told our driver we needed to go and would he please shave our heads? He was calm. He said he had to stop and get a new pair of scissors. Amazingly enough, no tourists were there except us. He cut our hair as short as possible, and then took us to a Balinese barber who finished the job.

I had suspected we had more "death urge" to process, and sure enough we did. Markus got bronchitis there and could barely make it up the 400 steps. When I got back home I got an abscess on my throat (fear of speaking out in Washington D.C.), and it took me nine days to clear it. Then the miracles started happing after we surrendered. A gal from Virginia who was a Babaji devotee was in Bali with us. She told us not to worry, she would find us the right apt. in D.C. We had other assignments and did not have time to go there and look, so that was amazing. She not only found us a beautiful apartment with fourteen foot high ceilings, she also found one in a great location just south of Capital Hill, the Navy Yard. It was later designated to be one of the "twelve coolest" neighborhoods in the world by Forbes Magazine (bit.ly/12Coolest). Not only did she find the apartment, she also stayed at our place and received all the boxes and unpacked everything. When we came to Washington D.C. after the India Quest in late March of 2017, our entire place was already fixed up and decorated by her. All our clothes were hanging in their closets, the furniture was well placed, and the kitchen was laid out perfectly. Another Babaji miracle. The only thing left was for Markus to hang the art—as she felt he would want to do this for himself, being an artist. We moved in and it was all done! Within a day we had all the artwork up.

So we said to Babaji, "What do you want us to do in Washington D.C.?" He said, "Nothing. Just be there and send your energy out." So that is what we are doing now—sending out the vibe of Truth, Simplicity, Love and Service in *The Perfection of Babaji*!

Love,

Sondra Ray

You Cannot "Make Me Up"

Since Babaji took conscious departure in 1984 I had not seen Him so often. However, my relationship with him deepened, and I would see Him approximately once a year in a vision or a dream. He told us that if we see Him in a dream or in a vision during a session, it meant He really came. You cannot make Him up, He said. I am not able to explain how this works. I often would see Him after completing writing projects.

After writing *Pure Joy*, in Australia, He was suddenly "there," instructing me to sit next to Him on His asan (holy seat). Then He materialized a ball of fire in His left hand and placed it on the ground at our feet.

After writing the first draft about my life (*There is A Cow in My Bathtub*—which is not published yet), He appeared as a King dressed in clothes made of jewels. The jewels were so "alive" and I saw them "breathing." He told me to come with Him for a ride in a chariot. We went down a secret road, and there was a palace made of "breathing jewels." It was alive and I was amazed that it could change size. Later I was writing a book on Physical Immortality that was mind blowing. I had put myself in seclusion and told no one what I was doing. I got a strange call from a lady in Hawaii I did not know—out of the blue. She said she was the wife of an astronaut and she told me to KEEP GOING on that book no matter what. How did THAT happen?

After finishing my first book on Physical Immortality in Hawaii, *How to Be Chic, Fabulous and Live Forever* (which was my first attempt to write a whole book on that subject), He appeared in miniature form only a few inches tall at my feet. He was totally complete and alive; but He was "pocket size."

Sometimes when I have been too blocked, He will appear to a clairvoyant in my vicinity and that person will call me to relay a message to me. Usually the person who sees Him is stunned by this, and their life begins to change as well. Once I had to have a surgery on my sinuses due to a severe infection. They had to scrape my sinus cavity out so the cilia would regrow. I was under anesthesia for quite some time, and the doctors marveled at the fact that I gave a lecture while asleep on "How the Atlanteans programmed the dolphins." I have no memory of this, but the doctors apparently went to get others to hear me. Post op was pretty hard. I played *Om Namaha Shivay* mantras to help get the anesthesia out of my body. A clairvoyant who I did not even know called me and said Babaji had appeared to her and there was a tree of life with avocados on it. Babaji plucked one off and was eating it. At that point I needed a tree of life.

One year I had a vision that I was on top of a very narrow mountain that was very hard to climb, and it was so thin that only two people could stand on the top. It was very hard to make it up there; and when I got to the top there was Shastriji, Babaji's High Priest (also a guru of mine) waiting for me. He began doing ceremonies with me and we did a special Aarti (the song we chant to Babaji every day in the temple, morning and night). Later, when I told Shastriji himself about this, he said that this was a turning point, and that I would now go through rapid spiritual changes. I could not imagine what that would be. I felt like I had been through so much already that I kind of wanted a break.

When I came back to the States, I began having very strange "episodes." For example, when my book *Inner Communion* came out, I had an intense reaction. My body felt like glass was shattering all through it. I could hardly stand up. My spiritual advisors told me that the old structure was breaking down. I went through temporary periods of old age, including something like rheumatism. I felt so strange it was something like what people who described bad trips on drugs. I would cry for hours on the floor in front of my altar. But then there was always a miracle: a healer would come into my life who knew what to do—a body worker, or a clairvoyant who would somehow understand. They would explain to me that my electromagnetic fields were being worked on; and that I was receiving "transcendent energy" from another dimension. Babaji would send me these healers.

What saved me was the certainty that by the grace of my Guru, through *The Perfection of Babaji*, I was being transformed into something new and going to a new level. Somehow I knew that Babaji was turning my life into something Divine. It was a mystery—all a mystery. But I knew that on the other side of these changes there was ecstasy, so I was always willing to go through them.

When I was longing for a mate, I told Babaji that I wanted Him to find me the right partner. That was because I knew I needed someone who would fit the mission. It could not be an ordinary man. I knew I could not attract the right one by my own thinking—what if I made a mistake? So I told Babaji to give me an "arranged marriage." It took a while. Once I was sitting in front of a clairvoyant in the UK and he told me that I was going to meet a man that I already knew. I told him that was impossible because I did not know any man who was free that would fit the mission. Then he told me he saw Babaji dancing around Ammachi (my female guru). He was thrilled with this vision. So was I, even though I still could not see who this man would be.

In the end, it turned out perfectly. Babaji kept his promise. Markus and I met in the winter of 2007-2008, after a twenty year period of not seeing each other. (He came with me to Babaji's ashram way back in 1987.) The words of the clairvoyant rang in my head, "it will be someone you already know." At first I did not believe it. And he was wearing a baseball cap which doesn't turn me on at all! And I met him in Philadelphia, not where I would have thought. But two of my European assistants, Diana from London and Shanti from Paris, said to me, "Are you crazy, he's the one!" We went for dinner with Shanti as my chaperone, and he gave me one of his journals to read. It had some little paintings in it that were just delightful, and some very deep writings alongside of them. Well, I got off it, and the rest is history !

The Master Is Beautiful

Sri Sri 1008 Haidakhan Babaji

by Markus Ray

What can one say about a Being who was not *born of a woman?* Who would believe that a Being manifested a body out of the light, out of thin air, so to speak, for the sole purpose of aiding humanity through these troubled times? Like the stories of old, He is similar (if not synonymous) to Melchizedek, "who had no father or no mother, but was a priest for all eternity." A being like Babaji is almost inhuman, but at the same time while incarnated in a body—*more human* that humans. His unconditional Love for humanity is unsurpassed. He is an Immortal Yogi of the Highest Order. It is even suggested that beings like Jesus Christ bowed at His feet, and received His instructions and blessings. Some say Babaji shaved Jesus's head (the spiritual purification practice called "mundan"), just before Jesus began His mission. You could dismiss all this as "new age" balderdash. You could. But you could also miss out on one of the greatest Blessings of Life, and the help of this Master of Masters to aid you in your ascent to being all you can be.

There is a famous phrase in the Catholic Mass, "Lamb of God, Who takes away the 'sins' of this earth, have mercy on us." Babaji gives us the ultimate mercy by pointing out there is no sin. Mistakes that need corrected and transmuted, yes, but 'sin' in the sense of an original "blight on the soul" of all humans—certainly not. You are born into original innocence, and this is what Babaji and all the spiritual Masters are here to restore to our awareness. We have defiled our own altars of Self-Identity, and They are here to help us *set right what is already right*. They come to remove the sorrow of the world, brought about by our own spiritual ignorance, and sense of separation from our very Source, our very Self—One of Pure Joy.

Babaji is so closely connected to this Source of Light that He can manifest a body from it, which He did most recently near a small remote village of Haidakhan in the foothills of the Himalayas in 1970. He has been around in some body—forever. He is also referred to in Yogananda's book, *Autobiography of a Yogi*, that speaks of an Immortal Yogi Christ of India in Chapters 33 and 34. You can read Yogananda's account of Babaji here online:

https://www.ananda.org/autobiography/#chap33

Yogananda writes this about Babaji in Chapter 33:

> *Babaji's' mission in India has been to assist prophets in carrying out their special dispensations. He thus qualifies for the scriptural classification of Maha-Avatar (Great Avatar). He has stated that he gave yoga initiation to Shankara, ancient founder of the Swami Order, and to Kabir, famous medieval saint. His chief nineteenth-century disciple was, as we know, Lahiri Mahasaya, revivalist of the lost Kriya art.*
>
> *The Mahavatar is in constant communion with Christ; together they send out vibrations of redemption, and have planned the spiritual technique of salvation for this age. The work of these two fully-illumined masters—one with the*

body, and one without it—is to inspire the nations to forsake suicidal wars, race hatreds, religious sectarianism, and the boomerang-evils of materialism. Babaji is well aware of the trend of modern times, especially of the influence and complexities of Western civilization, and realizes the necessity of spreading the self-liberations of yoga equally in the West and in the East.

1. From Light Out Of A Cave

In 1970 an unprecedented event occurred in a small cave at the base of Old Mount Kailash near the remote mountain village of Haidakhan (often called Herakhan) as mentioned above. A young man, looking to be in his late teens, early twenties, manifested a body out of the ethers. You're going to say, "No way. Someone's fantasy; totally made up!" Nevertheless, in spite of your objections, there were eyewitness accounts of this miraculous occurrence. What ensued was equally remarkable.

After manifesting his body in the cave, he climbed to the top of Old Mount Kailash and sat for 45 days and nights in silent meditation without sleeping, eating, drinking, or relieving Himself. Others who met Him in this period saw constant visions of their past lives flash before them. The intensity of His gaze was too much for most people, so He kept his eyes closed and gave people blessings with simple hand gestures—or *mudras*.

In the beginning of His mission he called His Indian devotees who gathered around Him and began the spiritual work that He initiated. A few years later He began calling his Western devotees who would be part of His world-wide extension.

You have to be determined to get to Haidakhan in the foothills of the Himalayas in Northern India. It is a journey to a place you may feel called. This in itself is an act of trust, because, like a mythical Shangri-lá, there is only an etheric substance to this place of calling that cannot fully be described with words. Only some inkling is drawing you, leading you forward into the Unknown. But this inkling is so strong, so undeniable as a force of direction, one can scarcely ignore it without feeling some great violation of Divine Destiny.

So you *get it together,* drop everything else, and just GO. In my case, and in the case of many others, I went with Sondra Ray, one of the principle Western devotees of Sri Babaji. I answered this calling back in 1987, and it continues to unfold in my life over 30 years later. I went on the India Quest (bit.ly/RayQuests) and I was glad I did, because the first time to India can be daunting, and the safety of a group of high-minded spiritual seekers provides a structure—a safety and structure that is helpful and needed. Sondra takes a group every year to participate in Navaratri, the Divine Mother festival. We go in the Spring when it is held in Haidakhan, Babaji's first home/ashram.

You take a plane to New Delhi, stay in a good hotel to rest and acclimate for a couple days, then take a 6-8 hour road trip to a small city, Haldwani, in the Nainital district of the state of Uttarakhand. A night in Haldwani prepares you for a jeep ride through the Kumaon Mountains the next day, which is unspeakably beautiful. A couple of hours of that, and you descend to the base of the mountains along the river bed of the Gautama Ganga, and voila!—you enter Haidakhan triumphant! That's pretty much how to get to Haidakhan from a logistical point of view. How to get there in your heart is another story. Best to know a little more about Sri Babaji to do that. He is a Master who calls the few, and you just may be one of them.

When Babaji rematerialized in 1970, His mission was all encompassing in this current age—but no less important in addressing the contemporary problems, both external and psychological, that we face in our everyday lives. Restoring a sense of the sacred; honoring the Elemental Forces of Life; bringing to awareness the Divine Feminine aspects of Creation; focusing the mind on a Divine Mantra (a true prayer); living by the virtues of Truth, Simplicity, Love and Service to humanity—all these served as the tenants of His teachings to the world. From His remote outpost in the Himalayan foothills, He drew to Himself the brightest and the best. It is even said that Steve Jobs paid Babaji a visit in His last materialization.

Sondra Ray and her Rebirthing teacher, Leonard Orr, met Babaji in 1977. They were some of the first Westerners to meet Him, when He began calling His non-Indian devotees. This meeting for Sondra began a long relationship with the Master. He is quoted as saying, "Rebirthing is the new Kriya Yoga. Westerners don't have the patience for long and involved meditations. They need something fast like Rebirthing." So began their quest to spread Rebirthing worldwide, which they did. Sondra has been travelling ever since around all parts of the globe spreading the good news about Babaji's teachings and the practice of Liberation Breathing / Rebirthing / Breathwork. Now it has "morphed" into many different names and approaches, but Sondra Ray is one of the original keepers of the process handed down to her from Sri Babaji in the 1970s. Go here for more info: bit.ly/LBSession.

Babaji gave what worked for people's spiritual evolution. He was not interested in empty rituals or belief systems that would add more to our conditioned brains. He wanted us to be free of this, and walk the life of Liberation. Like all Maha Avatars, He taught through the vibrations of His own lofty Being, and often in Silence, or in an exchange of Energy that transcended words. Being in the Presence of Him was enough to transform anyone who remained open for this transformation. He took people who were blocked in the illusion of their false selves, and turned them into masters of their broader and enlightened destiny. He was the Great Ganesh, the remover of obstacles. He was the Lord Shiva, who could destroy our ignorance. He was the Divine Mother, who could restore order to the elemental aspects of our planet earth.

Many bowed at the feet of this Master. It is said that Babaji was the "Guru of Gurus." In other words, many who came to Him were already teachers in their own right, but needed another step even higher. So Babaji cleared them of their Karma and limitations still left to remove in this lifetime, thus making their missions in the world more true and effective.

2. *Truth, Simplicity, Love and Service*

Babaji did not give long discourses. He did not put forth complicated programs of spiritual practices requiring His students to push themselves with severe austerities of renunciation. His teachings were very straightforward and streamlined: "Work is worship," He said, "and idleness is death!" Babaji stressed what is called Karma Yoga, which is the yoga of work, of action, of what one does to be productive—and to dedicate work to Service and Divine Gratitude for Life. Babaji wanted people to evolve, and face themselves. He aided everyone in their process of undoing, and subsequently their spiritual awakening—but He never made anyone dependent on Him as their sole source of impetus, growth and inner transformation.

Inspiration is to be found in the potentials within each one of us. It is our own inner work that all of us have to do. Can we release our stress, our impurities, our fears and disfunctions that are holding us back from being all we can be? Babaji gives us the inner clarity to do so. And then in the space of this inner clarity, we Serve, we Love, we keep our life Simple, and we always speak our Truth no matter what it may seem to cost us. The real cost is keeping our impurities. It is no real cost to be our true Self. One must struggle hard and pay dearly to keep his illusions.

The evolution of our soul is our responsibility, with the aid of the Master. They cannot do the inner work for us; they merely point the way. We have to take our own steps.

We have to undertake the arduous process of letting go of our ego for the emptiness and freedom of our Higher Self.

In the Presence of a Master Teacher, however, a person is brought to total attention. There is a feeling one is exposed, totally seen, totally understood. So if there are feelings of inadequacy in us, we will feel this experience of inadequacy in the Presence of a Master Teacher—for the purpose of release. Sondra Ray has a saying:

Love brings up anything unlike itself for the purpose of healing and release.

The Master is pure Love, therefore He or She is going to bring up in us anything unlike Love—a sense of inadequacy, not feeling good enough, anger, insecurity, doubt, confusion, feeling generally lost, etc.—all *for the purpose of healing and release.*

This is usually what happens when we meet a Spiritual Master. We feel incredibly exposed, like the Master can *see right through us.* Well, all of our shadows come up because the Master does *see right through us.* But this is a good thing. How can inner impurities be released without first coming to the surface?

Babaji knew that this internal cleansing is necessary for any soul. In fact this is why the soul incarnates here in the first place—to mend, to correct, to evolve, and to be a more full and loving human being. The importance of a Master in our life is to cut time and speed up this evolutionary and correction process. The Master sees in us what we may not see in ourselves. He or She sees our impurities, but He also sees our God created grandeur. And on this vision of our grandeur, the Master sets His sight to lift us out of the quagmire of our past errors, tendencies, and mistakes. He renders these mistakes ineffectual, with no more consequences. But we have to surrender to this process of spiritual purification. This is the Grace of the Master. He can take us farther along our evolutionary path than we could have gone alone. He can help us to undo the *little self* we made-up in exchange for the grandeur of the Self God created. He can speed up our process, and compassionately cut time for us.

He can introduce us to our real Self in no time!

As I said, Babaji did not give long discourses. *Truth, Simplicity, Love and Service* form the four pillars of His teachings. Truth is not only consistency of our words with the facts, and with our deeds, but it is also in owning the subtle ways in which we may be deceiving ourselves with anger, judgments, egoism, selfishness, and all the other impurities—pride, greed, jealousy, lust, attachment, envy, etc. The Truth is here to clean these things up. The Truth is here to undo all of these personal conditionings.

Simplicity was explained to me by a yogi in India as "Living within your means." Do not waste, do not indulge in the unnecessary. Be living a life in which all you have is purposeful for your mission in this life. Give yourself leisure and the pleasurable things that come with that, but always be in balance with work and worship. Love is knowing we are one with God, and that our needs are being met, and we have a surplus of abundance to give to others. We are courageous, and charitable. We see the others in our life as opportunities for us to give and serve.

Service to humanity is supreme. The real purpose of life, after we have "cleaned up our act," so to speak, is to serve humanity. This is the function of real Self-Mastery. This does not mean we "sacrifice ourselves." It means we engage in work that we love so much that it becomes a holy act for us. It brings us so much JOY we cannot wait to do it, and then we want to extend this Joy through giving it away. And this is Service. We Serve the greater good by first serving the higher Self in us.

Genuine Service will always produce Pure Joy in the Server, which then is extended to the recipient of the Service. Gratitude is inherent in this kind of Life Action. I am grateful for the privilege to Serve. Are you? It comes automatically, so I do not need "acknowledgment" from those whom I serve; I know my Service is being well received, and God knows what I am doing. So who needs to have their horn tooted?

The reward from Service is in the giving itself. Once that takes place, we become a juggernaut of the Good, without even having a motive to do so. It just becomes natural to us. We are doing what we love more than anything else, and our extension of this action meets the practical, emotional, and spiritual needs of others. That is Service. That is Loving. That is Simple. And that is True.

Writing this book, *The Master is Beautiful*, is just such an Action of Service for me. I am sharing what I love, which is writing to convey the Presence of the Masters Whom have so much graced my Life. In writing this book, They Grace you as well.

3. Earth, Air, Fire, Water, and Space

Babaji worked with the elements: Earth, Air, Fire, Water, and Space. This is to say He worked with the Divine Mother. The Divine Mother is the physical manifestation of the Universe. Nothing takes shape in Life without its birthing into being through the Divine Mother Herself. She is the Force of Nature that gives everything a place in the Cosmos. She is Nature Herself, in all Her palpable manifestations and in all of Her mysterious manifestations. As we would say, there is nowhere God is not, we would also say there is nothing the Divine Mother did not manifest. She is the Feminine aspect of God Whom brings form to the formless. She takes the Divine Father's loving idea and constructs it, atom by atom, into an entire COSMOS. To Her we pay homage, as did Babaji, Her Son, through honoring the building blocks of Her Universe, Her elements—Earth, Air, Fire, Water and Space.

Babaji was consistent with this. Every day He would build a fire and make his offerings to the Mother. Every day he would bathe in the waters of the Gautama Ganga River, and breathe in the clear mountain air in the midst of Haidakhan. Every day He would walk upon the ground of the earth and give thanks. He filled His space with gladness and gratitude, and He extended this Pure Joy to all who came to meet Him. He was Himself a manifestation of the Divine Mother, and He had absolute certainty of that. His Divine connection was unprecedented and elevated to the extent people lives were transformed by His mere gaze; He was the embodiment of fire which could burn away our ills and impurities in a matter of a few moments.

I could wax on to enlarge this picture. There is a place in Haidakhan that is unspeakably beautiful. It is called Babaji's Kutir, which are the rooms that compose His living quarters. During His last manifestation from 1970 to 1984, He occupied these rooms.

Under two huge bodhi trees, overlooking the river valley below, Babaji had a Havan, which is a specifically built fire pit, just outside of his bedroom. Every morning He would arise, have His bath in the holy waters, then sit at the fire and make offerings and prayers to the Divine Mother. All the elements would be honored. All the universe would be kept in balance by His action of this Divine offering and homage. Some have said without the great Yogis of the Himalayas performing these services to the Divine Mother, our planet would have got so far out of whack by the egotistic behavior of man, that we would have even more chaos than we have now. Only through the Grace of beings like Babaji, and their diligent spiritual practices, do we maintain even the slightest semblance of order in our human affairs. We could believe this or not. I choose to believe it.

Every year we take a group of spiritual aspirants to Haidakhan. We go in the spring for Navaratri, which is a nine-day, nine-night festival devoted to the Divine Mother. It is an intense program of paying homage to the elements, as Babaji did so well, in ceremonies that stretch throughout the day from 4AM to 9PM. There are prayers and songs sung in the temple. There are rites of offerings to the Divine Mother and Babaji. There is a Fire Ceremony, called a Yagya, every late morning for nine days straight. This fire ceremony is the crux of the festivities. People gather around it, and offerings are made. Ancient mantras are recited, and the people are uplifted into a vortex of Sacred Thanksgiving. The intensity of the blessings transcend the physical plane, and bring forth a sense of well-being, community, harmony and peace for the entire Cosmos. One can certainly feel the gratitude building inside—just to be alive. This is the power of Babaji, and these are the elements He brings back to our awareness, which sustain and bless us constantly—all of our Life. Join us on an India Quest. Go to: www.bit.ly/QuestsRay for more Info.

Love,

Markus Ray

From the book ***The Master is Beautiful*** by Markus Ray (bit.ly/MasterRay)

Meeting A Spiritual Master Like Babaji

I was very fortunate to meet Babaji and spend time with Him on several occasions. For me there is only before Babaji—and after Babaji. He totally turned my life around. I became a different person. For example, I was a nurse when I first met Him and I had no idea I could be a public speaker and a writer. He turned me into that. At the ashram, He would suddenly shout at me, "You—give a speech~!" I had not a moment to prepare, and I was mildly terrified. He did this enough to me though, and I got used to it. He was seeing my future. My major book on Babaji I wrote is ***Babaji, My Miraculous Meetings with a***

Maha Avatar, as well as 23 others over the years. If you read that book on Babaji, you will get a real sense of how He works with people, and how He worked with me. These are wild and entertaining stories—and all true! You can get this book here: www.bit.ly/BabajiRay. It also contains the specific teachings of Babaji, which you will find very important and practical.

The most valuable benefit from a spiritual Master is the awakening of an absolute state of mind: having absolute love, absolute peace, absolute happiness, absolute joy is our natural state of being. It is not natural to be in a state of duress and ridden with problems. A spiritual Master helps us to erase them and to return to the peace of our Divine Self. This relationship in our life is more valuable than any other. Nothing else would compare to its worth. Having this relationship is a great gift of life and it leads to complete satisfaction. The Master changes the literal physics of your level of existence at the level of mind, the level of energy, the level of light. You are very, very fortunate to find this kind of Teacher. He or she is your direct channel to God. Usually the meeting was pre-ordained and arranged in the soul world. It is an inconceivable leap in evolution. This relationship changes your nervous system, chemistry of the body and structural functioning of the brain. This shift would more accurately be called a *transmutation.*

The guru's love will intoxicate you. Slowly your love becomes so intense that the craving to be loved by the Master turns into craving to be in loving service to humanity. It is possible then to be in the promised land where you find love everywhere and you are literally walking on an ocean of love. Worship is the highest non-judgmental form of absolute Love. If we worship our Master (and all humanity through Him) we will learn very quickly and completely. In this state of being, *the Master Is Beautiful* because He or She extends into everything in our life!

When the Master has worked on our ego, the ego becomes useful to the world. Our ego becomes a tool for our Higher Self. Our characteristics will be refined and well molded; and by the Master's grace, our ego will be well under control. We will be fearless. Then the Master can work through us. The Master's Presence in us is a never ending stream of Divine Energy.

The Master also helps us heal our wounds and remove our pain. The Master will make us *look at it*. How can we remove our hidden pain if we are not even aware of its presence? If we let Him or Her work on us, we will be given the anesthesia (His or Her unconditional Love) so we can take it, tend to it, and heal it (whatever "it" is). The Master will not leave us stranded in the middle of a process. When the master begins to operate on us, He won't let us go when the operation is only half over. He completes the procedure. The Master's intension is to give us permanent relief.

If we don't have a Master, we might stray in the wrong direction. There is the possibility of falling. Is there any work we can learn, and learn well, without the help of a teacher? It is, then, best to receive the guidance from someone who has completed the journey. The Master offers everything He or She has to the disciple, and expects nothing in return. A Satguru (translated *true teacher*) is the fastest vehicle for taking us to our goal. If our goal is God-realization, which it probably is if you got this far in reading this book, then I'll tell you the truth—the Satguru is needed. Following any path without the help of the Satguru is like traveling in a shuttle service bus which will have a hundred stops and not even get you there in the end. This will delay your process. Being with a Satguru is like traveling in a Concorde Jet, faster than your spiritual journey has ever gone before toward a true promised land. And—it is super-sonic, at warp speed!

A true Master is a PRESENCE, the Presence of Divine Consciousness. He does nothing. In His Presence, everything just happens—without any effort on His part. It is the most conductive atmosphere for opening of our heart. We can pour our heart out to our Master. For years I have always written letters to Babaji and placed them under my altar cloth where I keep His picture. It always works! I call out to Him with any problem. Only a Satguru (Self-realized Master) can bestow the necessary grace, energy, and create the right conditions for our total liberation. Only in the Presence of the Self-realized Master can total transformation really take place. You can have this relationship now. You don't need to wait to have a "meeting in the flesh." Markus has given you enough in his book, ***The Master Is Beautiful***, to begin your journey relating to these incredible God-lit Souls. That is the purpose of his book, and I think it is true to that purpose. You can find it here: bit.ly/MasterRay.

Reading and holding a book like this on Spiritual Masters is like having a communion with them. Their living presence lives in these accounts of their purpose, sharing, and teachings. We are delighted that you can also have *The Perfection of Babaji* in your life through this short little book that describes Him and His most profound impressions He made upon us.

Love,

Sondra Ray

The Perfection of the Aarti

The Aarti is a song sung in Temples all over India. And the Haidakhan Aarti is particular to Babaji, though it also has some words and phrases common to all Aartis sung in India. The Yogis who wrote it down saw the words in golden brilliance descending from the heavenly realms in the ethers, and then they wrote them down as received. The Aarti is also considered "an offering of the lights." So, whenever it is sung, the Temple Priests share a small offering of open flames to the people. They take the lit lamp around to the congregation of people, and people waft the light from the fire over themselves. In this way it is like a "communion" of Babaji's Light coming to us. You could even light a candle when you are reading this book, and this chapter, to receive the full benefit. Here is the Haidakhan Aarti in English. It is good to read a few lines and then meditate on their meaning. In this way you make direct contact with *The Perfection of Babaji.*

Haidakhan Aarti

The Guru is Brahma, the Guru is Visha,
the Guru is Lord Shiva;
the Guru is verily the Absolute One.
That is why I bow to the holy Guru.

The image of the Guru
is the root of meditation.
His feet are the root of worship.
The speech of the Guru
is the root of mantras.
The grace of the Guru
is the root of liberation.
Endless like the shape of the circle
encompassing the whole dynamic

and static universe,
to Him who shows us that abode of God,
to that Guru I bow.

O Lord, sitting in the perfect pose,
residing in solitude,
Thou, Lord, ocean of knowledge full of bliss
of peaceful nature, pure and generous,
Thou gives us liberation !
Hail, Hail, O King of Sages
who removes the pain of His devotees.

Thy form is white and beautiful,
Thy smiling holy face is like a lotus,
Thy broad forehead has a third eye
with very brilliant light,
Thy big eyes overflow with tears of love.
Hail, Hail, King of Sages
Who removes the pain of His devotees.

In the darkness of illusion
I do not see Thy form;
In times of calamity

I don't remember Thy name,
nor have I ever worshipped
Thy holy feet that remove illusion.
Hail, Hail, King of Sages
Who removes the pain of His devotees.

Thy greatness, like the endless sky,
is told on earth;
Thy famous grandeur and sweetness
reverberate everywhere;
O Lord who gives liberation,
Have mercy on us.
Hail, Hail, King of Sages
Who removes the pain of His devotees.

Residing peacefully
on the beautiful mount Kailash
is that Sage whose form
always radiates compassion.
To Him I constantly bow.

By whose mere remembrance
a devotee gains perfection,
to the ultimate Guru who resides

in Haidakhan, to that One I bow.

By whose merciful look
people become liberated,
to His feet I constantly bow.

I bow to Him whose heart is soft,
Whose speech is soft,
even Whose correction is soft,
Whose body is soft.
Thy vision is full of mercy—
How it sees the moving
and non-moving universe;
how it is always busy
doing good in the world.
Thou are free from attachment and jealousy.

Supreme Guru, basis of all good qualities
Whose true meaning is hard to reach,
through meditation on eternal Truth,
Consciousness and Bliss,
I always remember Thee.

Thou are Vishnu Himself,
as well as a devotee of God.
Constantly meditating on God,
by drinking the nectar of God's name
one attains God's holy eternal abode.

Thou gives to the ignorant
true knowledge very difficult to attain.
I am without any spiritual practice;
Thou art my only refuge.
Thou are great like the sun
dispelling the darkness of illusion.

Thou art in the soul of all beings,
Immersed in the very life of Mahendra, Thy
Great Devotee.
I bow to thee, O Lord, image of mercy;
To Shiva Who is affectionate to His disciples,
doer of goodness,
destroyer of death and suffering—
to the incarnation of compassion,
I always surrender.

This is full, that is full;
from perfection comes perfection;
take away perfection and only
perfection remains.
OM, Peace, Peace, Peace.

Praise to the holy Lord of Haidakhan !
Victory to the great King !
Shri Mahendra Maharaj, the great master,
Praise to the eternal sacred Haidakhan !
Victory to Shiva, Lord of Kashi
and to Shri Kalbhairav;
Praise to the universal mother Amba;
Praise to the Divine Mother of Haidakhan;
Praise to Hanuman;

Praise to the Eternal Religion;
Let there be victory of righteousness;
May unrighteousness be destroyed;
Let all living beings have good thoughts;
May the whole universe be benefitted !

Praise to the river Gautama Ganga,
Praise to the river Narmada,

Praise to the Jata Shankara,
I bow to the Lord of Parvati !

Praise to Om,
The ultimate Guru Shiva Shankara,
always united with the Divine Mother Amba !
Vishnu Om !

O Lord Shiva Shankara—
You are the image of mercy,
then why do you delay so long?
Remove poverty, suffering and doubts;
Have mercy, have mercy.

Restless and saddened
by the cares of this world,
O Lord, I have fallen at Thy lotus feet.
O Lord of the three worlds, save me now;
Have mercy , have mercy.

Thou art beautiful with
Thy body covered with ash;
Lord of this world, Lord of the universe,
half of Thy body is the beautiful

Mother Goddess Amba—
Lord of the Mountains,
Lord of the Ganges,
with the crescent moon on Thy head,
Thou art the image of peace.
Lord of the people, Lord of my being,
Remove poverty, suffering and doubts;
Have mercy, have mercy.
Who does not know
Thy motherly love for Thy devotees?
But I am not even a real devotee of Thine.
I truly must admit this:
I do not rely on my devotion to Thee,
but on Your grace only, O Lord.
Remember Thy promise,
Have mercy, have mercy.

Thou art the Lord of the universe;
then why should I turn to somebody else?
Thou art the sustainer of creation;
then what could I gain from others?
Thou alone art in my thoughts
and my actions;
then what could I take from anyone else?

Thou art the God of gods;
then why should I weep in front of others?
Have mercy, have mercy.

Ramana, Thou art easily pleased—
this way of being pleased is unusual.
All beauty adorns Thee;
Thy form is worthy of being worshipped;
Thou art a storehouse of energy;
Thou art great and powerful;
Thou art knowledge and beauty,
Always busy in benefitting us.
Have mercy, have mercy.

Thou art a constant spring of bliss,
the infinite essence of truth.
Thou art form and the base of everything,
pervading the whole material world.
Thou art worthy of being served
by Lakshmi and Vishnu,
yet Thou art Their selfless servant.
The reward of divine love comes
to those alone who always repeat Thy name.
Have mercy, have mercy.

Who has been able to know so far
the greatness of Thy name?
Gods and demons alike sing
Thy name until today,
trusting that Thou and Thy name
shall constantly reside in my breath !
Have mercy , have mercy.
Holy Master, Thou give only grace;
Shower grace on me, have mercy on me.

O Lord, Thou art brother of the humble,
giver of everything;
Shower grace on me, have mercy on me.

Thou art the Trinity,
knowledge, knower and object of knowledge.
Shower grace on me, have mercy on me.

Holy Divine Master, Thy eternal form
is the embodiment of joy !
Shower grace on me, have mercy on me;
Have mercy , have mercy.

Embodiment of the bliss of the Absolute,
bestower of the highest joy—
Thou art knowledge personified
beyond duality, formless like the sky.
Thou art that goal of all goals,
the object of proclamations
such as the one Absolute, eternal,
pure and immovable Being.

You are the witness of all intellects
beyond thought and the three gunas;
to Thee, Supreme Guru, I bow.
I have taken shelter in Thee,
O Lord of Haidakhan;
Thy names are the supreme Guru.
Thou art the remover of sorrows, and
I have taken shelter in Thee.

Lord, Thy pure nature is full of compassion;
when will Thou show compassion to me?
O destroyer of pain,
I have taken shelter in Thee.

O Lord, on that day Thou makes me Thy
Own now, what can go wrong for me?
O Remover of my misfortunes,
I have taken shelter in Thee.

The mind of the devotee is limited;
Thou art the great perfect Lord.
Teach me an easy spiritual practice,
O One of Your peaceful countenance !
I have taken shelter in Thee.

How can I describe Thy endless greatness ?
Show Thyself to me, O mighty armed one.
I have taken shelter in Thee.
Thy face is full of radiant light;
Thou art the personification of bliss;
Let us hear Thy sweet voice—
O One of priceless speech.
I have taken shelter in Thee.

Thine merciful eyes are a source of beauty.
In them there is no poison or discrimination.
Thou art known as the one of equal vision.
I have taken shelter in Thee.

Utter the name of Haidakhandi !
Speak of God, Truth, Consciousness and
Bliss. Proclaim holy Samba Sada Shiva !
Shiva unites with the Mother Amba,
Sustainer, Inspirer, Master of the world.

Hail, Hail to the Lord residing in Haidakhan,
Who embodied for liberation of the world.
Thou alone are my true Divine Master,
Invisible unperceivable Shiva,
the ultimate God—
Shri Haidakhandi !

Thy heart is full of mercy.
The one who surrenders to Thee
is immediately liberated.
What pain is there in the world which cannot
be instantly removed by Thy grace ?
O King of Sages,
Shri Haidakhandi !

Thou always speak words
which remove our fear;
Baba fulfills all desires.

O Lord, Thou art the source of
auspiciousness and the remover of evil.
Lord, I surrender everything at Thy lotus feet.
Shri Haidakhandi !

Great sage of sweet speech,
Thou art extremely benevolent;
Thy sentences are
the very essence of knowledge;
the true eternal religion, full of generosity,
tells of knowledge joined with pure action.
Shri Haidakhandi !

Thou gives to each one
his own honorable duty;
Jealousy and hatred are not called
rightful actions;
Truth , Simplicity, Love and Service;
O Brother, this rule alone brings
happiness to man.
Shri Haidakhandi !

Repeat the Lord's name, O Brother,
to purify yourself and find the

Lord sitting in your heart;
Holy Shiva is residing in the unity of your
heart—recognize Him and renounce
ignorance and disappointment.
Shri Haidakhandi !

Great Saint, the ocean of all qualities,
whose beginning and end nobody knows,
resides in You.
Haidakhan is Your quaint abode,
giving endless joy and solace.
Shri Haidakhandi !

The river Gautama Ganga
is roaring day and night;
Saints, gods and demons
worship there every day;
Looking at the beauty of
Holy Mount Kailash, the seeds
of longing sprout in the mind.
Shri Haidakhandi !

Under Mount Kailash
there is a beautiful cave; that

great cave is described in the Vedas.
The forest animals and deer
roaming in the dense woods
spontaneously forget hostility
among each other.
Shri Haidakhandi !

Since the Lord started living there,
the beauty of Vrindavan, the garden of
Heaven has faded in comparison.
Blessed, blessed, blessed is this holy
pilgrimage of ours to Haidakhan,
where the embodied Shiva enjoys living.
Shri Haidakhandi !

Thy merciful look gives us love
for Thy holy feet.
By no other means can one get a pure mind
now Lord, show me Thy grace this way,
and let me renounce all things, and
sing Your praises day and night !
Shri Haidakhandi !

Praise to Amba, Mother of the Universe,
Mother Goddess Amba,
Thou art the One in all forms !
Shri Haidakhandi !

BOOKS by SONDRA RAY & MARKUS RAY

LATELY I'VE BEEN THINKING: POWERFUL POSTS ♪ FOR AN AWESOME LIFE

Relationships expert and spiritual mentor, Sondra Ray, brings her wisdom to Facebook with daily posts written over a period of two years. These tidbits of advice uplift and enlighten us on many common life subjects—from finding your life's purpose to discovering your formula for happiness. Markus Ray, Sondra's twin flame, compiled these short entries to bring you these powerful ♪ posts for an awesome life.

Do you find yourself reading short snippets these days? In the Facebook and Twitter millennium, sound bites and staccato posts hit the points of our attention like quick fixes of cappuccino stops at Starbucks. A half a page is about all we can handle with our morning latte. Here is a mélange of morsels of wisdom to ponder over your morning brew. With skill and prowess to get to the point in vernacular language, Sondra Ray brings us "Lately I've Been Thinking," her essential commentaries on just about everything in life you will encounter. For any age or gender preference, delve into these "Powerful ♪ Posts for an Awesome Life" and get your jitterbug juices flowing toward nirvana.

AMAZON LINK: www.bit.ly/LatelyRay

ALPHA OMEGA

The companion to SONDRA RAY's **Lately I've Been Thinking**, Markus Ray compliments his wife's free flowing commentaries on Liberation Breathing / Breathwork, A Course in Miracles, Holy Relationships, and wisdom for day-to-day living. These guides for various Spiritual Quests to Sacred Sites around the world, continue their prolific output of written roadmaps to purposeful living.

Do you ever have a "dialogue" with yourself? Have you ever kept an ongoing journal of your everyday observations? Is your "start" and "finish" so intertwined they meld into just one thing of Pure Joy? ALPHA OMEGA is just that from MARKUS RAY— painter, author, and poet of "Odes to the Divine Mother." These journal entries from 2006 to 2009 form the basis of his commentaries on A Course in Miracles, his relationships with the Spiritual Masters, various life issues we all face, and his inner preparation to join with SONDRA RAY, his "twin flame," with whom together form the duo of a Holy Relationship. In this New Millennium made manifest, ALPHA OMEGA is a daily companion of freewheeling meditations, and a compendium of insightful tidbits that will tweak anyone's awareness of the First and the Last lesson of the Absolute in our everyday life.

AMAZON LINK: www.bit.ly/AORay

LIBERATION: FREEDOM FROM YOUR BIGGEST BLOCK TO PURE JOY

What is your biggest block to having Happiness all of the time? What's keeping you in a polite hell? Why has your life fallen short of Heaven on Earth? This book by Sondra Ray and Markus Ray will answer these questions for you, and provide the thread out of the labyrinth of your most negative thoughts in your subconscious that are sabotaging your life, or preventing you from going all the way to Pure Joy. Discover what they call a "Personal Lie," that is your most negative belief about yourself, hidden in the deep recesses of your psyche. Everyone has one to overcome. It is a main cause of all the things and events that went wrong in your life. Free yourself from it by reading this book, and practicing a few forgiveness processes.

AMAZON LINK: www.bit.ly/LibRay

THE MASTER IS BEAUTIFUL

THIS IS A BOOK for you to have holy relationships directly with Spiritual Masters in your life. Do you want them? Markus Ray presents 9 parts in this book, each dedicated to a Spiritual Master who has greatly contributed to the eternal Wisdom of human spiritual evolution. He makes these Masters and their messages very accessible to the general public, in a way that can endear them to anyone interested in transforming themselves "upward" in their process of enlightenment.

Who would you invite to a holy banquet of the Wise? What would be your short list of dignified guests who had contributed the most to the enlightenment of your life? Author and artist Markus Ray puts together his exclusive "Master list" of those invited to his "last supper" of Spiritual Wisdom. You are invited too. Wouldn't you like to participate in this celebration of the best and the brightest? Come along with Markus on this insightful journey to the feast of Absolute Love from these remarkable Beings.

AMAZON LINK: www.bit.ly/MasterRay

I DESERVE LOVE

This book can clear up your sex life—totally—and infuse new Joy into your sensuality! You Deserve the Perfect Lover, and Sondra Ray tells you how to find and win that person. You need only decide what would make you completely happy in a relationship and you can achieve it, quickly and without struggle. The Power to get what you want is within you, and you can tap into it through the simple affirmations set forth in this dynamic book. Sondra Ray explains simply and clearly how to use the tested affirmations exercises, how to adapt them to your specific needs, and how to put them to immediate use. If it sounds too easy, read the many case histories that demonstrate their effectiveness. Then prove it to yourself—put affirmations to work in your own life!

The Rainbow Millennium is a whole new section added to the second edition of this popular book, dealing with the LGBT community, Sex after 60, and the new millennium attitudes of a shift—further opening the door for innocence and acceptance to enter our views on sexuality.

AMAZON LINK: www.bit.ly/DeserveRay

PHYSICAL IMMORTALITY: HOW TO OVERCOME DEATH

This is a book that can permanently lift you out of despair, depression and hopelessness—a book that shows you how longevity is the linear result of quantum living.

Humans have something buried inside of them called an "unconscious death urge" which is our secret desire to destroy a body we feel trapped in. In this groundbreaking book, Sondra Ray teaches you how to dismantle the unconscious and hypnotic program (the unconscious death urge) which is literally killing you. The real tragedy of the unconscious death urge is not only that it causes us to die before our time, but that it generates a resistance-to-life of pure JOY. It makes life less attractive and therefore intensifies our desire to die and put an end to our misery. It's a vicious cycle.

This book is the solution that is 100% affirmative of life that offers a viable alternative.

AMAZON LINK: www.bit.ly/LiberationRay

THE NEW LOVING RELATIONSHIPS BOOK

Working through the depths of self-awareness using affirmations and emotional exercises, this book shows that loving relationships begin with self-love. Ray demonstrates how to find, achieve, and maintain deeper, more fulfilling relationships.

Revitalize what it means to be in a Loving Relationship. You are meant to be in heaven, here and now, with your mate. This book is a roadmap for a new loving relationship in the 21st century which puts you there. Learn what it means to have a "conflict-free" relationship that is liberated from limitations and strife. Learn what it feels like to be free of old paradigms our parents were stuck in for years. Save decades of time and get clear that you deserve Pure Joy ! Get the basics, which are all the beatitudes of gratitude that take you higher and higher in your Love together.

AMAZON LINK: www.bit.ly/NLRBRay

BABAJI: MY MIRACULOUS MEETINGS WITH A MAHA AVATAR

This book may just blow you mind. The wild stories of a wild woman meeting her wild Guru in 1977, and all the stories of subsequent meetings afterwards. Unbelievable and true—off the charts encounters with Babaji, the Maha Avatar first mentioned in Yogananda's Autobiography of a Yogi in chapters 33 & 34—but in real life, in real time with Sondra Ray.

In her usual provocative style, Sondra asks her readers

●What if you could know a Being who is not born of a woman and who could dematerialize and rematerialize his body? ● What if you could know a Being who is a major teacher of Jesus and who prepared him for his mission? ● What if you could know a Being who knows everything about your past, present and future? ● What if you could know a Being who is the bestower of the highest Joy? ● What if you could know a Being who incarnated for the liberation of the world? ● What if you could know a Being who would fulfill all your desires?

You can know Him. This book is about Him. He says to you, "My Love is available. You can take it or not." Why not take it?

AMAZON LINK: www.bit.ly/BabajiRay

What people really want in their relationships is deep connection, good communication, and spiritual intimacy. Sondra Ray and Markus Ray explore these common desires. They also give you 18 good ingredients that establish spiritual intimacy. And these ingredients permeate into all areas of your life, and transform them to embody truth, simplicity and love throughout.

Whether you are in a relationship or you are searching for that "right person," join Sondra and Markus to receive the benefits of living in the sacred zone of Spiritual Intimacy, What You Really Want with a Mate. Spiritual practices can get you in touch with your divine nature and help you stay clear of conflict and problems. Sondra and Markus give you simple approaches for integrating your spiritual life into your love life, leading to the possibility of Pure Joy! Examine the importance of Spiritual Intimacy in all aspects of your life—sex, money, parenting, career, and family life. Discover how true forgiveness, *A Course in Miracles*, and Liberation Breathing® combine to help you release the old paradigm that sabotaged your life in the past. Sondra Ray, the "Mother of Rebirthing", reveals how your birth trauma may be affecting your relationships, and what you need to do to clear it. Liberation Breathing® is an experience every person or couple should try!

AMAZON LINK: www.bit.ly/IntimacyRay

ODES TO THE DIVINE MOTHER

Through intimate portraits and inspired meditations, Markus Ray cracks open the sacredness in coffee cups, mountaintops, airports, and vistas to reveal a Source that is divinely feminine. Infused with the essence of his lifelong study of *A Course in Miracles*, each page explores topics from ego and forgiveness to joy, Holy relationships, and Christ consciousness through daily dialogue with the Divine Mother. A sacred stillness emerges as one's consciousness opens—line by line to the purity, power, love, and perfection that is the Divine Feminine.

Markus Ray is a visionary painter, poet and teacher. He lives in Washington, DC, with his wife, author Sondra Ray. Together they offer seminars, virtual programs and Quests to sacred locations around the world, introducing thousands each year to Liberation Breathing®, The Loving Relationships Training®, and A Course in Miracles. Markus is the coauthor of Liberation Breathing: The Divine Mother's Gift. His paintings are featured at www.MarkusRay.com. Also see Markus Ray on Art Look —an art lover's companion— at www.bit.ly/ArtLook

AMAZON LINK: www.bit.ly/OdesRay

LITTLE GANESH BOOK

Solve all you problems with this book! In this collection of short aphorisms and meditations, Markus Ray pays homage to Ganesh—the Elephant God in Eastern mythology Who is the remover of obstacles. You can use them to inspire your day, and to remove the difficult hurdles in your own life.

A friend gave Markus a tiny Ganesh and he immediately loved it as it is pocket size. Therefore Markus always carries it with him. Knowing that Ganesh is the one who removes obstacles, I have seen Markus take it out of his pocket and set it on the counter, especially at airports. This was funny because I usually had my suitcases overweight so Markus was asking Ganesh to "handle that." I must say it very often worked! Ganesh is the Lord of success and destroyer of obstacles. This is the most popular deity in India. His large belly is an essential attribute. It is said to contain within all the universes, past, present and future. There are many legends as to why Ganesh has an elephant head. One explained that Ganesh was created by Shiva's laughter.
—Sondra Ray—

AMAZON LINK: www.bit.ly/GaneshRay

LIBERATION BREATHING: THE DIVINE MOTHER'S GIFT

This is Sondra Ray's "Bible on Breathwork"—a guidebook for expanding into life, spirit, and happiness through the power of your own breath. Discover how Liberation Breathing -- a form of breathwork practiced worldwide—transforms on the mental, physical, and spiritual dimensions. Sondra Ray's newest book on Breathwork elevates the soul while releasing readers from negative thoughts, traumas, and relationship patterns. Ray unites the power of breath with her extraordinary commitment to healing and miracles as she details the evolution of Liberation Breathing. She reveals how the breath cycle transforms the mind, body, and soul when coupled with self-inquiry, prayer, and affirmations. Through essays and case studies, she details the spiritual and historical influences of the modality while honoring its roots in the Rebirthing Movement. An instructor manual for breathwork practitioners, a guide for birth workers, and a rich source of information for those seeking personal transformation, this book is for anyone intrigued by the benefits of conscious, connected breathing. Sondra Ray and Markus Ray merge their collective knowledge of breathwork with their passion for *A Course in Miracles* and the Divine to bring you the most salient teachings of the past 40 years.

AMAZON LINK: www.bit.ly/LiberationRay

MIRACLES WITH MY MASTER, TARA SINGH

In this book, author MARKUS RAY comes forward to transmit to you the many blessings he received from his teacher of "A Course in Miracles," TARA SINGH. This touching story of miracles, raising the dead, meeting the saints of India is compellingly and openly told within. MARKUS spent seventeen years studying with TARA SINGH from Easter of 1989 to March of 2006 , and describes him as, "my life teacher, my spiritual guide, my Master, and my friend." TARA SINGH was guided directly and ordained by the scribe of "A Course in Miracles", Dr. Helen Schucman, to give workshops and instruct serious students of this sacred, self-awakening course for enlightenment. His insights into the application of ACIM's principles stand unrivaled, as written in "A Gift For All Mankind," one of his major classics.

MARKUS says, "I wrote this account of those years I spent with TARA SINGH—our encounters, his teachings in my life, our travels and experiences together at home and abroad, and my own melding with the Presence of this great man—so other students of ACIM may receive the intensity of actual miracles in their study of this modern day scripture. Also, I desired to write an accurate complement to TARA SINGH's mission with ACIM, seen through the eyes of one of his students."

AMAZON LINK: www.bit.ly/TSRay

ROCK YOUR WORLD WITH THE DIVINE MOTHER

"Those who explored the frontiers of universal spiritual consciousness were true pioneers. Their ideas were mind blowing and life altering for an entire generation, for whom such beliefs were startlingly outside the box. One of those pioneers was Sondra Ray.... If Sondra writes a new book, I read it. I let go of my left brain and drink her in, imagining her sitting on a chair, explaining to me what to her is so obvious and the rest of us, well, maybe not so much. I have never experienced Sondra as anything other than a beam of light.... I have lived enough to be able to say that of all the good fortunes I have had in my life, encountering her has been one of the liveliest. Sondra Ray is more than a woman.....The word GODDESS comes to mind...." —Marianne Williamson—

My favorite part is the 108 Names of Divine Mother puja. Sondra Ray clearly knows her subject, which is her close relationship with the female aspect of God. She is definitely a powerful Divine Mother channel! —Linda Smith—

This book has the markings of one written by a mystic. The language is poetic, transcendent and full of grace. Sondra's gentle words will help you connect with the Great Mother energies! This is one of my favorite books ever. —Jacqueline Moss—

AMAZON LINK: www.bit.ly/MotherRay

PELE'S WISH

"Pele's Wish continues the bold, wonderful saga of Sondra Ray's journey into Spirit. She makes everything we long for seem so possible. We are very lucky to have her in our midst." —Marianne Williamson—

With her kitchen-table style storytelling, first-hand adventures, ancient poetry and song, and practical spiritual exercises, acclaimed new age author Sondra Ray uncovers another side of Hawaii that outsiders rarely see or truly understand: The wisdom and spirituality of the Hawaiian ancients and their kahuna wisdom. In Pele's Wish, Ray acts as a messenger of the Aloha spirit with the teachings of the Kahunas, or "transmitters of secrets" with her personal guide, Maui-based kahuna Auntie Pua. The ancient rituals and basic tenets of the "Huna" way, loving yourself, nurturing other beings, the land, and living in harmony with all of life, is shared in Ray's conversational, accessible style with meditations and practical exercises to bring the spirit of Aloha into our everyday lives. You don't have to be Hawaiian to benefit from this ancient wisdom, wisdom that can lead to eternal life!

Ray reveals a time-tested practical code leading to a deeper spiritual life, in tune with rhythms of the natural world.

AMAZON LINK: www.bit.ly/PeleRay

HEALING AND HOLINESS

Are you going through a rough time? Or are you are concerned about someone in crisis in your life? This book is for you. Respected author, teacher, and nurse turned metaphysical healer Sondra Ray shares her spiritual and physical journey in HEALING AND HOLINESS. Written as an intimate personal testimony, Sondra tells of her struggles-toiling through difficult exercises with her spiritual masters—and her triumphs—experiencing the transformative powers of rebirthing and metaphysical healing—as she learns to recondition her mind and body to heal with and without using Western medicine. Originally released under the title HEALING WITH SONDRA RAY, this edition offers new insight into the workings of the unconscious mind and our ability to affect the way the mind controls the body. HEALING AND HOLINESS is destined to become one of Sondra Ray's most important and beloved books.

AMAZON LINK: www.bit.ly/HolinessRay

THE LOVING RELATIONSHIPS TREASURY

Collected from her groundbreaking series of relationship books, THE LOVING RELATIONSHIPS TREASURY distills the core teachings of Sondra Ray's unique approach to finding, achieving, and maintaining the deepest, most fulfilling relationships possible. Ray's timeless writing continues to inspire us to begin our personal journeys toward integrating intimacy and spirituality within every significant relationship—with ourselves, our mates, our parents, our children, our colleagues, our world.

What others are saying about this book:

Author talks about the inner workings of the body's energy channels and how to achieve. Great book to study constantly. Thumbs up on this book. —Robert T. Lewanski—

I loved this book. Very insightful and spoke to my soul. I especially loved how the author combined therapy with meditation. —L. MacAdams—

AMAZON LINK: www.bit.lyTreasuryRay

ESSAYS ON CREATING SACRED RELATIONSHIPS

CREATING SACRED RELATIONSHIPS is as much an intimate look at the woman behind the teaching as it is the culmination of her most recent spiritual initiations and encounters. Sondra Ray's riveting personal story is presented along with a collection of essays that inform, inspire, and promote the conscious exploration of new means and methods by which we may journey towards new relationships with ourselves, our mates, our business associates—our world. This gathering of thoughts explores nothing less than the creation of a new model for all our relationships. And this model is a manifestation of our own personal "heaven on earth."

AMAZON LINK: www.bit.ly/EssaysRay

INTERLUDES WITH THE GODS

In this account of Spiritual Masters who touched and shaped her life, Sondra Ray gives us a glimpse of some of the most off the chart meetings and impressions of these Holy Beings who represent the top shelf of human evolution. The list is not exhaustive by any means, but her descriptions of God-Like Beings she has met in her life gives us a kind of litmus test to find our own pantheon of enlightened beings to guide us as well. Writing in her crystal clear vernacular style, Sondra gives us a blessing—a simple stroke of a divine caress in these various "Interludes with the Gods."

AMAZON LINK: www.bit.ly/InterludesRay

INNER COMMUNION

Here the author of Loving Relationships shares her special insights about the importance of spiritual nourishment of the self and one's relationships—the inner communion that can be achieved by opening up to the lessons of life and love. The finer nuances of spiritual nourishment are explored here in Sondra Ray's inspiring look at "communion." Nurturing ourselves through the experience of inner spiritual states leads us to richer relationships with ourselves, with others, and with God. Personal and touching, this book looks at communion from many aspects—from the strictly religious to the broader communion of intimate relationships and our place in the fabric of being.

A special chapter narrates Sondra's profound pilgrimage to Croatia (then Yugoslavia), where the apparition of the Virgin Mary made itself known to thousands of devotees in Medjugorje in recent years. Her story is both fascinating and deeply moving.

AMAZON LINK: www.bit.ly/CommunionRay

HOW TO BE CHIC, FABULOUS AND LIVE FOREVER

Sondra Ray's first book that considers the possibility of immortality, argues that one should be the most important, celebrated, and fashionable person in one's life, and tells how to take advantage of all life has to offer. What people are saying about this book:

Sondra provides a wonderfully concise and comprehensive text for anyone wishing to fully embark on a mind-body approach to healing and wellness. Her enthusiasm speaks through the text, and she provides many specific methods across different parts of one's life to cultivate emotional-spiritual wellbeing, referencing a plethora of other texts in the process that can allow her readers to continue their path to immortality through their own investigation and practice. If nothing else, her book validates the obviously essential act of cultivating beauty in everyday life, without fear. —Amazon Customer—

I'm reading and old copy of this mind-blowing book by Sondra Ray. How to Be Chic Fabulous, and Live Forever is about immortality and even though the Bible talks about immortality, I gave little thought to the idea that I might actually be able to live for as long as I want or need to in this Earth suit. But this topic (along with ascension into a light body) has been on my mind recently. —Yvonne Perry—

AMAZON LINK: www.bit.ly/FabulousRay

PURE JOY

Life can be filled with Pure Joy and Love, and there are many spiritual practices, thoughts, and sacred texts to help us find that joy. Here the author of *Loving Relationships* and *The Only Diet There Is* shares her discoveries of the many spiritual practices available to help us in our ascension upward on our life journey—practices learned during Sondra's life-long spiritual quest and leadership, and on her incredible spiritual Quests to India and beyond.

In addition to Sondra's inspirational writing, *Pure Joy* also contains essays written by staffers of the Loving Relationships Training, offering additional insights and guidance on ways to find and maintain a life filled with Love and Joy at its purest.

AMAZON LINK: www.bit.ly/PureRay

BIRTH AND RELATIONSHIPS

Did you ever think the circumstances at your birth could affect the rest of your life? Did you ever wonder if being induced made you not trust authority? Does difficulty completing things relate to being a cesarean delivery? Do you do things backwards because you were breech coming out of the womb? These are questions Sondra Ray asks and answers in this groundbreaking work on how your birth script affects your life and relationships.

Co-authored with Bob Mandel, Sondra Ray does the groundbreaking work of studying how the type of birth you had influences your personality, your relationships and your whole life; How your birth script – namely conception, prenatal period , delivery and postpartum – impacts the decisions you make in your life and especially in relationships. She also writes on how to heal the trauma of birth and early childhood, and get clear that your "birth script" is important to understand and unravel in order to have a more free and unlimited life.

AMAZON LINK: www.bit.ly/BirthRay

IDEAL BIRTH

Sondra Ray lays out the truth about giving birth, and takes the courageous road to introduce birthing practices that are enlightened—namely, underwater birth. She fills in the blanks and takes the mystique out of what should be a natural celebration and easy transition—not a "traumatic labor." This book will break the whole mindset of the medical model that grips women into a fear based and primarily patriarchal leftover from the days of Kings and male dominated obstetrics.

What people are saying about this book:

I gobbled this book up! I followed the guidance for talking to my son while he was still percolating in the womb, and used many of her suggested resources to understand my child's womb experience more fully. The book also set me up to give birth to my son underwater, which was a wonderful experience. I relied heavily on the guidance from Sondra Ray. —April Shoemaker— Empowering Parenting Coach

There's LOTS of books out there on having a baby but so very few of them center on how the child will go through the birth process and what the CHILD feels and experiences. This book helps you to consider giving both the mother and the CHILD an experience that is profound and POSITIVE.—Anna—

AMAZON LINK: www.bit.ly/IdealRay

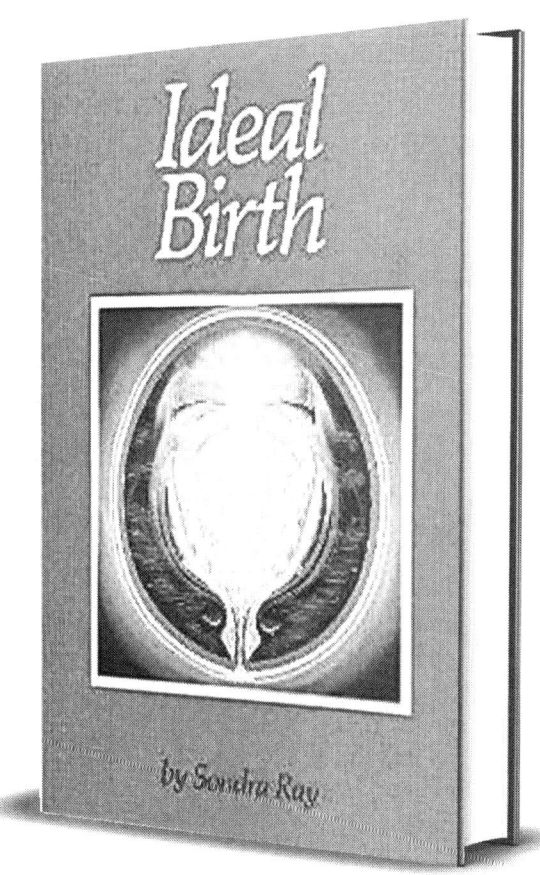

DRINKING THE DIVINE

This book is for people interested in, or studying "A Course In Miracles." ACIM is a magnificent spiritual work that has brought many people to inner peace. "Drinking The Divine" provides a beautiful summary of the key points in the text section of ACIM. It is set up to be a one year workbook, providing a guide to the serious student of ACIM for learning the entire course over a one year period. ACIM stresses release of guilt through growth in forgiveness in its teachings. Drinking the Divine by Sondra Ray is recommended highly for its WONDERFUL summaries of the text section of ACIM. Readers have found them extremely helpful in guiding their understanding of what the text says. The text of ACIM is very abstract and is difficult to grasp in spots, and these summaries are extremely helpful to the new student of ACIM.

AMAZON LINK: www.bit.ly/DrinkingRay

CELEBRATION OF BREATH

In this second primer on Rebirthing, Sondra Ray further elaborates on the effectiveness of Breathwork to change your life for the better. Basically this book introduces people to the process of deep, circular connected energy breathing, in order to release stored subconscious memories that are hanging us up in life. This book discusses how to have well-being, physical perfection, healing and longevity by using Rebirthing/Breathwork.

What people are saying about this book:

I love this book, since 1980s, the second from Sondra Ray on Rebirthing which i began in late '70s healing my deep birth trauma gradually in layers over decades. It's more feminine & sensitive than other rebirthing books, that appeal to your mind & healing needs. But Rebirthing, self-healing was/is slandered by normal psychology & shrinks calling the deep memories 'false memory syndrome' of birth or childhood. "Rebirthing" is both consciousness raising of being born again in the spirit of love now, & a deep conscious breathing systems; it can takes many sessions, years or lifetimes of deep work healing oneself. —Michael Sprague—

AMAZON LINK: www.bit.ly/CelebrationRay

THE ONLY DIET THERE IS

Here is a book to change your life. It is a method for losing weight through positive thinking and the changing of attitudes toward life and food.

This, of course, is no ordinary 'diet' book...This is an extraordinary approach to weight loss--a diet of forgiveness, a fast from negative thought--and if followed one can achieve bodily perfection. The theory is simple. Though we might think it is our negative eating habits that have kept us unattractive and unhealthy, it is really our negative thoughts and feelings. It is the latter we must change for that is what is aging and killing us. If we do...we drop our fat as well, for the same mechanism that holds on to negative thoughts and feelings holds on to fat.—from the Preface

AMAZON LINK: www.bit.ly/DietRay

LOVING RELATIONSHIPS I

This easy to read book uses ideas and philosophies from Werner Erhard's EST training, Ernest Holmes' Religious Science, Rebirthing, Affirmations, as well as cognitive and traditional modes of psychotherapy to give the reader new insights into the nature of love relationships. Techniques and ideas are given in workbook style to help one to improve and create successful relationships. Not for those who "pretend" to be open minded or prefer to blame the circumstances of their life on others. Not the standard "self-help" book that seems to find its way on to so many people's book shelves but not into their lives. Perfect for those who have completed the Landmark training, The Forum or Life Spring etc., as well as those folks who practice Religious Science, Unity or any other of the "New Thought" faiths. Equally helpful to those who have not participated in any of the above... I loved it and am buying extra copies for those I love. ★★★★★

AMAZON LINK: bit.ly/LovingRay1

LOVING RELATIONSHIPS II

In LOVING RELATIONSHIPS II, Sondra Ray continues the journey she began with the publication of LOVING RELATIONSHIPS I in 1980. This entirely new book shares her discoveries and adventures as she investigates deeper into the secrets of love, life, and spirituality.

What People are Saying About This Book:

I have read other Sondra Ray books and this one is the best... My husband and I were ready to divorce, A friend suggested this book, by the time we finished reading it we had a better perspective on the things we were doing every day to damage our own relationship and were able to get back on track. I recommend this book for anyone because it can improve even the best relationship.

An oldie, but a goodie! Loving Relationships I puts into words many things that I have contemplated myself - my reactions and responses to many things and to many people in my life. Loving Relationships II is even better! Addressing both the past and present, it gives us a tangible understanding of how to deal with and resolve conflict within our lives. A definite breath of fresh air, the book gives us permission to be ourselves. After reading this book, I wanted to love myself and others more. Thank you, Sondra!

AMAZON LINK: bit.ly/LovingRay2

REBIRTHING IN THE NEW AGE

Co-authored with Leonard Orr, this was Sondra Ray's first "manual" for the process of Rebirthing—the conscious, connected circular energy breathing that was innovated by Leonard and her in the early 1970's in San Francisco. The clearing of negative subconscious memories all the way back to a person's birth through this deep "breathwork" is first clarified in this book. Understand and get clear of "the five biggies" which are the main consciousness blocks to experiencing Pure Joy in your life. Learn how your breath is the interface between your conscious mind and subconscious mind, and can get you in touch with your super conscious mind which invokes metaphysical and spiritual solutions to you problems. Breath out the memories stored in the cells from your "birth trauma." Understand the "unconscious death urge" and why it is important to question the thought "death is inevitable."

AMAZON LINK: www.bit.ly/RebirthingRay

I DESERVE LOVE (First Edition)

This is the first book Sondra Ray published back in 1976. It is a classic book on the New Thought Movement, one of the first of its kind that made it clear that thoughts and feelings precede and determine all experiences. Before "Affirmations" was a household word, Sondra Ray wrote—*I Deserve Love.*

What people are saying about this classic, even 30 years after its original publication:

I have taken workshops and seminars from Sondra Ray as well as her "Loving Relationships Training". In my early stages of seeking to live more freely, through these books and Sondra—as well as her recommendations for further "self- work," I began to lighten up, live more feeling like "myself." Now, over 30 years later, I recommend these books and this work to ANYONE seeking self-awareness and growth! — Reverend Frank—

This book was published decades ago and was way ahead of everyone else in this field—maybe she invented the field of thinking yourself toward a goal. I now use it when coaching others on falling in love, relationships, etc. Affirmations with actions, that is the key. This book has power, real power. I used it thirty years ago to find a new relationship, told friends about it and they had the same results. —Morning Hill Walker—

AMAZON LINK: www.bit.ly/IDeserveLove

SONDRA RAY'S Author's Portal :

www.bit.ly/SondraRay

MARKUS RAY'S Author's Portal :

www.bit.ly/MarkusRay

Resources

Sondra Ray / – author, teacher, Rebirther, creator of the Loving Relationships Training®, Co-founder of Liberation Breathing® and Quests to Sacred Sites around the world.
Facebook: www.facebook.com/sondra.ray.90
Facebook Fan Page:
www.facebook.com/LiberationBreathing
Twitter: www.twitter.com/SondraRay1008
YouTube: www.youtube.com/SondraRay
Website: www.sondraray.com
E-mail: contact@sondraray.com

Markus Ray / – poet, author, artist, Rebirther, presenter of *A Course in Miracles*, co-founder of Liberation Breathing®,
Facebook:
www.facebook.com/markus.ray.169
Facebook Fan Page:
www.facebook.com/LiberationBreathing
Twitter: www.twitter.com/MarkusRay1008

Website: www.markusray.com
E-mail: contact@markusray.com

Receive Markus's weekly articles on ART:

"Art Look" - an art lovers companion -
www.markusray.com

Immortal Ray Productions
Nashville   Washington D.C.

301 Tingey Street, SE, #338
Washington D.C. 20003

See Sondra Ray & Markus Ray Here:

www.sondraray.com
www.markusray.com
www.facebook.com/LiberationBreathing

We encourage you, our reader, to attend *The Loving Relationships Training* (LRT) which is produced by Immortal Ray Productions all over the world. You can see Sondra Ray & Markus Ray's worldwide teaching schedule:

www.sondraray.com/programs-seminars

Also, we encourage you to attend The INDIA QUEST, The BALI QUEST, or other Spiritual QUESTS that teach and disseminate Liberation Breathing practices, and principles of *A Course in Miracles*, as well as enhance your Divine Connection to various Spiritual Masters. These are also available on: ***www.bit.ly/QuestsRay***

Artwork and paintings of the Spiritual Masters by Markus Ray are available on: ***www.markusray.com***

Liberation Breathing® Sessions

with SONDRA RAY & MARKUS RAY

Book a Session at bit.ly/LBSession

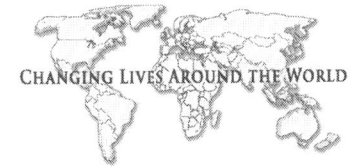

CHANGING LIVES AROUND THE WORLD

DEC. 3 – DEC 13 – EVERY YEAR

RETURN TO THE DIVINE MOTHER IN BALI, THE ISLAND OF THE GODS, AND THE WORSHIP OF THE SACRED FEMININE !

Join SONDRA RAY on her BALI QUEST, an exquisite journey of the soul to this ancient holy culture.

BALI QUEST with SONDRA RAY

ARRIVE: DEC 3
DEPART: DEC 13
EVERY YEAR

- **JOIN SONDRA RAY** in this life changing event. Journey to **BALI,** one of the most special places on the planet. Discover your sacred Self at most holy **Besakih Mother Temple.**

- Pay homage to the Divine Mother of all LIFE in BALI, and usher in 2019 at one of the "Immortality Power Points". Stretch your mind and open your heart on this profound journey. Visit the sacred waters of **Pura Tirta Empul Temple.**

- Arrive in Bali on DEC 3rd and meet the "Mother of Rebirthing", **SONDRA RAY,** to begin this quest of spiritual awakening through **Liberation Breathing®** from the Divine Mother. Witness **Gamelan Music & Balinese Dancing.** Soak up the rich Balinese culture that for centuries has worshipped the Divine Mother in practices of unrivaled beauty and grace.

- Total cost of the Bali Quest is $3500 US. ($3000 for Early Reg. Before Sept 1.) This includes transfers to the beautiful **Nefatari Villas of Ubud,** double and quad villa occupancy in traditional Balinese settings, Balinese cuisine, some planned excursions, and Bali Quest training tuition.
- **Register Here**: https://sondraray.com/programs-quests/
- Only 25 Spaces available.
- Email <contact@sondraray.com> for info and program.

Contact: <contact@sondraray.com> or MARKUS RAY at <manmohan1008@gmail.com>

For more info on SONDRA RAY : < https://sondraray.com/ >

Made in the USA
San Bernardino, CA
28 January 2020